Windsurfing Technique

Nikolaus Stickl/Michael Garff

Windsurfing Technique

STANFORD MARITIME

The techniques for learning windsurfing are described in this book. There are, however, more and more questions relating to the physical, biological and scientific interrelations of windsurfing, which interest the experienced sailors today. In order to explore these themes, four specialists were asked to write on their particular aspects of windsurfing for this book.

The analysis of the aerodynamics, the sail's cross-section and the forces on the sail and board was done by MICHAEL NISSEN, who is a sailmaker and a computer specialist for North Sails.

The exceptionally important function of the senses of equilibrium was described by TILO SCHNECKEN-BURGER, a former European Windsurfing Champion. Schneckenburger's description was adapted from his sport instructor's diploma dissertation.

HOLE RÖSSLER is a certified sports instructor at the Sports Institute of the Technical University in Munich. He explains the interaction between body stance and force transfer.

The chapter on the special techniques of wave-jumping and trapeze surfing was written by another expert, KARL MESSMER, several times European and World Champion.

Stanford Maritime Limited
Member Company of the George Philip Group
12–14 Long Acre   London WC2E 9LP
Editor Phoebe Mason

First published in Great Britain 1981
English edition © Bucheim Editions SA
and Stanford Maritime Ltd 1981
Translated into English by Judit Farkas

Reprinted 1982, 1983

Originally published as *Windsurfing Technik*
© Bucheim Editions SA, Fribourg 1981

Set in 11/12 Monophoto Univers 689 by
Tameside Filmsetting Ltd, Ashton-under-Lyne,
Lancashire
Printed in W.-Germany
G. J. Manz Aktiengesellschaft München-Dillingen/Do.

British Library Cataloguing in Publication Data
Stickl, Niko
    Windsurfing technique.
    1. Windsurfing
    I. Title   II. Garff, Michael
    III. Windsurfing. *English*
    797.1'24   GV811.63.W56

ISBN 0–540–07407–1

CONTENTS

RACING   133

TRICK SAILING   159

WINDSURFING PHOTOGRAPHY   165

THE OLYMPIC BOARD   172

CHAMPIONSHIPS   173

Open Class, Windsurfer, Windglider and Sea Panther

ACKNOWLEDGEMENTS   177

INTRODUCTION

No sport has come even close to windsurfing in experiencing such sweeping growth and development in such a short time. After its beginnings in the United States, Europe was overtaken by a boom. At present there are approximately one million people on the lakes and coasts of Scandinavia, Germany, Holland and France who are familiar with at least the basic principles of the sport. Its introduction into the British Isles followed the wave of popularity on the Continent, but in the last couple of years windsurfing, also known as boardsailing, has become a major growth sport there, attracting both non-sailors and those who were already familiar with dinghies and larger boats.

A look back to the beginning. The Californian engineer Jim Drake, an enthusiastic sailor, solved the problem of how to sail on a surfboard in an ingenious way, with a universal joint at the mast foot and a wishbone rig. To help him in the project, Drake got Hoyle Schweitzer involved financially. Schweitzer subsequently acquired the rights to the invention and is today, through patents and licences, the biggest beneficiary.

The Windsurfer, as the result of Drake's work was named, was produced for the first time in California during the late 1960s. A few of these models soon came to Germany, to the beaches of Sylt on the North Sea coast. Once it became apparent that the sport would not be merely a passing novelty, it became more organized, with sailing schools teaching beginners and later others, and clubs which held regattas and competitions for particular classes. After a few trials, the establishment of a Windsurfer Class, and other classes, began to succeed. The definition of permissible limits of critical shapes and dimensions of the board and rig allowed boards from different manufacturers and private builders to compete against each other in the so-called Open Class, which carries a large O on the sail. This attracts growing interest as the number of more advanced boardsailors grows, and from commercial manufacturers as it encourages experimentation and changes in design, and the development of short-run or prototype boards to suit specific conditions, weights and experts. Racing in the one-design classes offer competition for those who prefer to buy standard production equipment, and boards which may be easier to sail and have a longer life on the second-hand market.

During the 1980 Summer Olympic Games in Moscow, the International Olympic Committee (IOC) decided to make boardsailing an additional discipline in the sailing programme for 1984, in Los Angeles. In November 1980 the International Yacht Racing Union (IYRU) selected the Windglider as the official Olympic board. Many of the enthusiasts would have perhaps preferred to see the Windsurfer chosen, because of its historical and sporting significance for the triangular Olympic courses in California. However, the very clever politics of the Osterman Company and the diplomatic behaviour of Hoyle Schweitzer made the choice of the Windglider easier, especially for the representatives of the Eastern bloc countries.

The Olympic competition will differ substantially from normal boardsailing racing. Under the usual rules there is one winner in each of the two to four weight classes. At the Olympic Games, however, only one class will be sent to the starting line, without any consideration of different body weights. The gold medal winner will win not only through his ability, but to a considerable extent as a result of favourable wind and sea conditions. For example, in light airs the lighter sailors will have a definite advantage. The venues for the Olympics are generally determined by factors which do not necessarily provide ideal or varied sailing conditions and this has been significant in the past.

A particular injustice has been meted out to the women, who have received no special status whatsoever and must race with the men. This ruling may have an influence on future regattas outside the Olympics. If it should turn out that the capabilities of the top-ranking female boardsailors really do not differ much from those of the men, there may well be only mixed races in the future, particularly in countries where the sport is well developed rather than in the early stages, where separate racing for women and young people makes sense.

Why has the sport of boardsailing become so successful in such a short time? There are several reasons.

—The possibility of transporting the board along with its accessories on top of a car, and the resulting mobility, represents a considerable advantage over traditional sailing.

—There are no docking or launching problems; nor any need for a trailer or mooring.

—Membership in a sailing club is not mandatory in order to be able to put one's board into the water.

—It is easy to find a place in the garage or attic for winter storage, and maintenance is minimal.

But these are only prerequisites for what is an attractively independent, simple and dynamic form of sailing.

Boardsailing schools have sprung up on practically every body of water that offers enough space and the right sort of conditions, and many dinghy sailing

Preparation for a race

schools have added it to their programmes. The fundamentals can generally be taught in around eight to ten hours. Right from the start, the beginner feels that he is progressing. The direct contact with water and wind quickly teaches one to anticipate the different forces involved.

The price of the complete equipment is comparable with what one invests for skiing or cycle racing, and the tuition period is shorter than for, say, tennis or skiing. However, one should not be tempted into making a hasty purchase. It may turn out by the next season that the materials and construction are not that durable, or that this year's hot design has been superceded. As one becomes more proficient, higher demands are placed on the board and rig. Thus one is confronted with the choice of buying good equipment immediately, or supplementing or replacing it later on.

This is particularly true of wetsuits. Exact fit and quality construction, combined with good material which gives enough insulation, has its price. When a less expensive suit comes apart, or fits poorly and cuts off the blood circulation to the arms, or when the thickness of the rubber is insufficient to protect against the cold, then it's not worth the little money that it cost. On the other hand, it's also unnecessary to pay large sums for stylish trends.

When purchasing a board, one should have a realistic idea of one's aspirations and potential achievement. Is it to be simply for occasional enjoyment or family sailing, or as a second boat, or does one have one's eyes on more ambitious goals like racing, at club or higher levels? Is it for the exhilaration and control of free-style or surf sailing?

The aspiring racer is already limited in his choice by the fact that there is competition at the national and international level in only a few one-design classes. At present these are primarily the Windsurfer, Windglider and Mistral, and, so far mainly in the U.K., the Sea Panther. Alongside these classes, the Open Class is gaining increasing attention and importance. However, competitive boards which are within the measurement limits of this class and also have a good chance of winning are not exactly inexpensive. The design characteristics of the top-ranked boards seldom allow them to be used as 'fun

Windsurfing history: Ammersee Regatta 1974

boards' as they tend to be less forgiving and more difficult to sail. On top of that, because of their light construction such boards are prone to damage. One can say that boardsailing competition in the Open Class is analogous to Formula 1 car racing in that the materials and construction are oriented completely to competition and have little relevance to the average user. The other racing classes take in popular all-round boards which can be sailed by the average person and are more durable.

The choice of a specific board should depend a great deal on its materials. In general, there are two materials used, polythene (polyethylene) and glass-fibre reinforced resin (fibreglass or GRP). Polythene is tough and stable, and especially suitable for boards which are subjected to rougher treatment,

whereas fibreglass is hard, brittle and breaks easily when the outer layer is not thick enough. Its advantage is that it is easy to work with and therefore the boards are cheaper; also fibreglass can be repaired fairly easily. In addition to these materials there are of course others such as ABS and ASA. These are synthetics that are particularly suited to heat-forming; the production methods vary from one manufacturer to another. Through a number of special techniques, different characteristics such as minimal weight, local stiffness or particular stability are achieved.

Those sailors who do not want to spend much time caring for and maintaining their boards may be interested in a new kind which recently appeared on the market — boards made of polythene foam, pro-

... and the World Championships in the Open Class in 1980 in Israel

Both pictures illustrate the development within a few years

duced in the manner of children's surfboards from a very light material. They are not fragile: the board can be thrown by the surf onto a rocky shore and hardly show it. Also, falling down onto this material is not quite as painful as on the conventional boards.

In addition to the big market for brand-name boards, there are a growing number of custom-made ones and their builders. These are handmade singly for particular purposes, and the user's weight and preferences. Most are colourfully painted, have foot straps or stirrups, and the dimensions and shape are designed for specific purposes such as surfing, wave-jumping or high-speed sailing. The large manufacturers have tuned into this trend and are likewise producing boards for such purposes, as well as for Open Class experts. Shapes are constantly being

modified through experimentation and experience and are still in a process of development, which offers encouragement to those who wish to try out their own design ideas.

Obviously the correct rig is necessary for the board, including a suitable sail, daggerboard and fin(s). Through the patenting of the original Windsurfer, certain markets are restricted, especially with regard to the mast pivot and wishbone design, and the complicated international legal picture has yet to be resolved.

Naturally, the sail, the propulsive force for the board, is particularly important. It is not easy, especially for the racer, to find the right sail in this confusing market. It is advisable to have at least two different-sized sails, for different wind strengths and in con-

sideration of the weight and capabilities of other members of the family. An all-round sail of approximately 4.4 m² area and one of 6.0 to 6.3 m² are useful; smaller sizes are available for children. Inexpensive all-round sails and the smaller storm sails are widely advertised in sailing magazines. If it doesn't bother one to flaunt an advertisement on the sail, and the class and racing rules permit, one can even save a bit of money by obtaining commercial 'sponsorship' in this way.

The authors' idea was to write a book which in addition to excellent action photographs contained a thorough and extensive section on theory, technique for beginners and advanced sailors, a chapter on racing, and finally an introduction to windsurfing photography.

Beginners should bear in mind that the purpose of this work is not to replace qualified instruction but as an aid to acquiring sound, correct technique. The second part is devoted to the advanced boardsailor and instructs him at a technically high level.

Niko Stickl, Windsurfer of the Year in 1979, brings us closer to the modern techniques in a striking way. Michael Garff took several hundred photos of him, and from these and his extensive library the best pictures were selected in order to make it possible for the reader to follow the sequence of movements down to the smallest detail. Thus a book was created which enthralls not only the beginner and the expert, but also fascinates everyone by its photos. The possibility of presenting a manoeuvre from different angles in sequential photos, and the repetition of important sequences, leads to better understanding and easier learning, and the mastery of even the most complicated manoeuvres.

Windsurfing or Boardsailing

by Tilo Schneckenburger

The equipment for boardsailing has been ingeniously reduced to the most basic and absolutely indispensable items. There is a board, a mast, a sail, a boom, a daggerboard and skeg, but no rigging for the mast, no complicated fittings, and what amazes the bystander above all, not even a rudder. Nevertheless, a sailboard is more manoeuvrable than a sailing boat, when expertly handled. Since the board and rig are not rigidly connected, the board itself cannot capsize like a sailing dinghy. One can also stop instantly from top speed by releasing the boom and letting the rig fall into the water, which causes a prompt braking action.

The chances of injuring oneself are small when compared to other sports which give a similar degree of exhilaration, such as skiing or hang gliding. However, this sport is not totally without risks to oneself or others if one doesn't observe a few rules and safety precautions. These will be explained in the section on 'Regulations and Code of Conduct'.

In traditional boats, steering is accomplished with a rudder and tiller, whereas in boardsailing it is done with the rig alone. When the sail is tilted back, the board heads up into the wind; if it is brought forward, the board bears off. In light breezes (Force 0–2) the sailor stands with his entire weight on the board and must hold the rig upright. It is this situation that the beginner is usually dealing with. However, in winds of more than Force 3, the sailor hangs on the wishbone and only supports a fraction of his weight directly on the board through his legs. The rig supports itself as well as a large part of his body weight by means of the wind pressure acting on the sail.

There is another distinct difference from traditional sailing. In a strong wind, a sailboat heels over to leeward until the force of the wind on the sail is just balanced by the righting tendency of the boat, which is determined by its buoyancy, hull shape and ballast or crew weight. However, a boardsailor must pull the sail over himself to windward, which creates a lifting force in addition to the driving force. It carries part of his body weight, so that the sailboard lies less deep in the water and thereby becomes faster. (Indeed, some high-performance boards actually sink under the weight of a person, and have to be moving in order to run on the surface.) Because of this ability to plane, under suitable conditions speeds can be achieved which have been unknown until now with traditional monohulled boats. The Dutchman Jaap van der Rest won the 1980 Windsurfing Speed Trials in Holland with a speed of 45.50 km/h (24.5 knots), on a special board in the class allowing up to 10 m^2 of sail area.

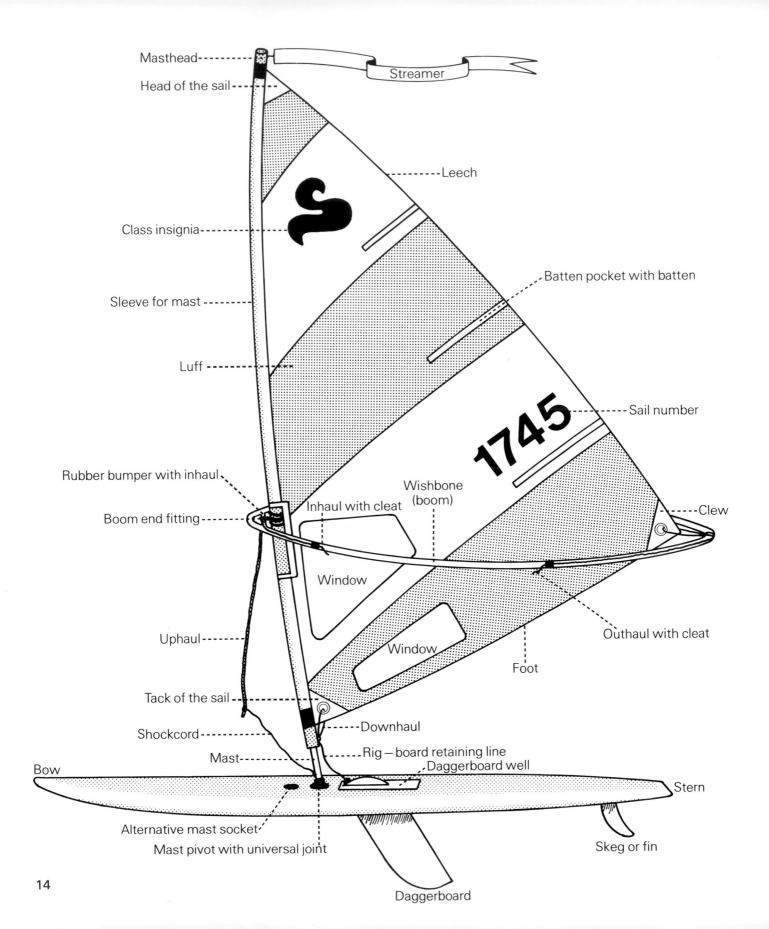

Masthead

Head of the sail

Streamer

Leech

Class insignia

Batten pocket with batten

Sleeve for mast

Luff

Sail number

1745

Rubber bumper with inhaul

Boom end fitting

Inhaul with cleat

Wishbone (boom)

Clew

Window

Uphaul

Outhaul with cleat

Window

Foot

Tack of the sail

Downhaul

Shockcord

Rig — board retaining line

Mast

Daggerboard well

Bow

Stern

Alternative mast socket

Mast pivot with universal joint

Skeg or fin

14

Daggerboard

Assembling the rig

The rig consists of the mast, a universal joint or mast pivot, wishbone or boom with outhaul and inhaul lines, and the sail. The mast is usually made of fibreglass or aluminium and is slid into the mast sleeve sewn into the sail's leading edge (luff). If the sail comes with battens, these should be placed in the corresponding pockets before setting. The tack (lower corner) is tightened with a short line on the mast foot, called the downhaul, tied with two or three half-hitches. The notch in the sail is necessary in order to be able to fasten the inhaul line (about 28 inches or 70 cm long) with a 'quick' inhaul tie or a mast hitch. This inhaul is tied tightly to the mast, making a flexible linkage that keeps the wishbone in position. Next, the other end is pushed through a hole in the front portion of the boom end fitting, then brought behind the mast through another hole in the fitting, and finally it is slipped through the cleat. The connection is secured with two half-hitches around the boom. The uphaul, for raising the rig, is attached to the front portion of the mast fitting and is a thick soft-textured line which is easy and comfortable to hold. A short elastic line on the lower end, which is hooked onto the downhaul or the mast pivot, keeps the uphaul always within easy reach.

Another method of fastening the wishbone to the mast is a clamp, which is capable of holding it at shoulder height under normal water and wind conditions, just like the inhaul. On the back (aft) end of the wishbone is the outhaul line, with which one can change the shape of the sail. When tightened, it pulls on the clew and stretches and flattens out the sail. The sail is set more loosely in a light wind, but still pulled back enough to get rid of the vertical folds at the luff when it is filled with wind. The sail shape and mast stiffness should be matched to each other since otherwise the tension on the outhaul and downhaul will be unequal and the sail's curvature less than optimal. The outhaul is brought forward from the boom end and through cleats.

Clothing

Depending on water and air temperature, and below about 75°F or 24°C, a neoprene wetsuit should be worn. Even in the sunshine, one can become chilled through over-exertion and the effect of constantly blowing wind. Short or long wetsuits are particularly necessary in our latitudes, and for the most part are provided for their pupils by windsurfing schools. Sailing shoes or sneakers give grip on the board, and protection from injuries on the sharp edges of boards and sharp stones, broken glass or rocky bottoms. Injuries from sea urchin spines, which break off in the skin, can be particularly uncomfortable and turn a vacation into torture. A securely gripping tread and a soft sole and ankle material make for good stability on the board.

A length of spare line and a knife, extra clothing, perhaps flares etc. can be carried in a small knapsack or a trapeze harness vest.

1

2

Knots

Two knots are used to connect the mast and the boom: the 'quick' inhaul tie, and the mast hitch or 'French' inhaul tie. Their function is to fix the boom to the mast at shoulder height and to hold it there so that it cannot slip down under strain. Otherwise, the sleeve in the sail which fits round the mast may be damaged. Check the condition of the inhaul line before tying the knots. Should it break when there is no replacement, it can lead to serious consequences, for example in an offshore wind or crowded waters. Paddling back can be very tiring if one is far from shore and practically impossible in a strong wind. Before starting out check all lines for strength and that they are properly fastened. One or two half-hitches in front of or behind the cleats will prevent the accidental release of the inhaul or outhaul.

5

6

3

4

'Quick' inhaul tie (1—4) A simple overhand or figure-of-eight knot on the end serves as a safety measure. A loop is formed, then laid around the mast and both the long and short ends are stuck through and pulled tight. Take care that the two ends do not cross.

Mast hitch (5—8) A simple knot is tied in one end of the inhaul, which becomes the short end. It is

wound twice around the mast and thereby crosses over the long end from below. After an additional turn over the long end, the knot is slipped under the last turn. The turns are pushed together and the slack is taken up by tugging back and forth on the long end. Since the wishbone is pulled downwards, one has to pay attention to the position of the knot on the mast. In picture 6 the direction of the pull is to the left.

7

8

The difference between a sailboard and a sailing boat is clearly seen here. In a strong breeze the boardsailor leans his sail towards the wind, to bring the forces on it and his body into balance.

TECHNIQUE I

The simulator

A dry land training board, called a simulator, is indispensable for efficient learning. Under the guidance of an instructor, this is used to help teach the manoeuvres of starting, changing direction, coming about and gybing. A tethered board, using a line through the daggerboard slot, is another safe and useful aid to learning, and enables one to practise balancing, and turning the board on the water with the feet.

Every beginner should pay attention to and concentrate on practising these basic movements, even if the urge to try everything out on the water is very strong.

The hand and foot positions will come up again and again later on and are the basis for getting moving easily, and sailing and steering freely and instinctively. In addition, it is easier to pull up the sail while standing on the simulator, and should one make a mistake one has only to jump off the board. On the water, however, a fall from the board is not always thought of as a welcome cooling-off.

Carrying the sail

The rigged sail is carried to the water horizontally over the head, with the luff of the sail (the edge along the mast) directed into the wind. One hand holds the mast above the wishbone, while the other supports the wishbone.

Next, the mast pivot is placed into its socket in the board and the retaining line is tightened to prevent the possible separation of the board and the rig. If there are several mast sockets on the board, in light wind the mast is placed farther back, closer to the daggerboard. In strong wind it should be placed farther forward in order to keep the windward helm

(the tendency to head up into the wind) from becoming too strong.

To tune up your sense of balance, do the following exercise before attaching the rig to the board. Bring the unrigged board to the water and first try to climb up and stand on it. This makes one realise that it is a rather wobbly affair. Balancing, rotating the body, and shifting foot positions and weight should then be practiced on the unrigged board in order to be able to make the correct reactions later on when the sail is being pulled up and the board is moving.

Pulling up the sail

For the first attempts at starting, the sail should be at right angles and on the leeward (downwind) side. In stronger winds the instructor will tether your board to the shore or a buoy with a line as long as the water is deep. This removes the risk of being blown away from the shore on open water, and the beginner has a chance to perfect on this 'floating simulator' everything he learned on land.

To pull up the sail, have it lying in the water at 90° to the board. The back foot rests between the slot and the foot of the mast, the front foot ahead of the mast. Straightening the body must be done so that the pull remains at a right angle to the board. By pulling harder with one hand or the other the board can be prevented from turning.

Pulling up the sail from the leeward side

Stand on the board on the windward side, gripping the uphaul line with both hands with your back to the wind. Pull the rig up part way by straightening the legs and upper torso from a slightly squatting position. The water will then run off the sail and it will become lighter. Then pull it all the way up hand-over-hand using the uphaul.

Important:

The back end of the wishbone must be clear of the water. While pulling up the sail it is also important to keep the position of the board and sail constant at right angles to the wind. The fluttering sail flies out to leeward (downwind) and indicates the wind direction. This position of the board, rig and sailor is known as the 'basic position'.

Should the first attempts end in falling and alter the position of the sail and board across the wind, one can correct this by pulling on the uphaul to either the right or left. One can always pull the sail up, regardless of its position relative to the wind direction, if the back end is allowed to swing freely and feather itself. While in the water, it only has to lie at a right angle to the board and then can stabilize it like an outrigger.

Raising the sail from the windward side

Occasionally the sail lies upwind of the board, as a result of a fall or if the wind has drifted the board around the sail. In order to be able to start from the basic position, the sail has to be brought round to the leeward side. Before pulling it up the board has to be aligned at right angles to it. The first phase of the

pulling corresponds to pulling it up from the lee side, but now the wind blows under the sail, lifts it up and reduces the tension on the uphaul.

The wind pushes the sail across over the bow, or as illustrated, over the back of the board. The sailor must move around the mast from the lee to the windward side, as shown, finishing in the basic position.

1

2

Raising the sail from the windward side

The sail is raised by stretching the legs and straightening the body, while the back is kept straight (1, 2).

After the water has run off, the wind gets under the sail and swings it around (3). Move around the front of the mast by taking small steps and pull the sail around over the stern with the help of the uphaul and the wind (4, 5).

Pulling hand-over-hand on the uphaul, raise the sail completely out of the water and take up the basic position (6).

In a strong wind this must be done much faster. The sail is blown across immediately from the windward to the leeward side, and the sailor must be just as quick in changing his position.

3

4

5

6

27

Rotating the board

To see how the board reacts to a movement of the rig before starting off, lean the sail sideways against the wind. This will turn it in exactly the opposite direction: as the board rotates, change position by taking small steps around the mast. The sail always remains on the lee side; the board is turned by transferring the wind's force onto the board, which is much faster and more effective than turning the board with the feet alone.

These photos illustrate a 360° counter-clockwise turn.

The first photo (opposite) starts with the mast vertical and the board in the '3:30 position' just below arrow 1, which shows the wind direction. The board is turned by first leaning the sail to the right. The sailor must change position by taking small steps around the mast as the board rotates. This illustration is meant to explain only the change of body position, how the sail is leaned toward the wind, and the corresponding reaction of the board. Normally, the board travels along a curve.

The next page shows how one can get into the basic position from the 'sail over the stern' position (1—6). The following photos demonstrate a subsequent 180° rotation of the board (6—12).

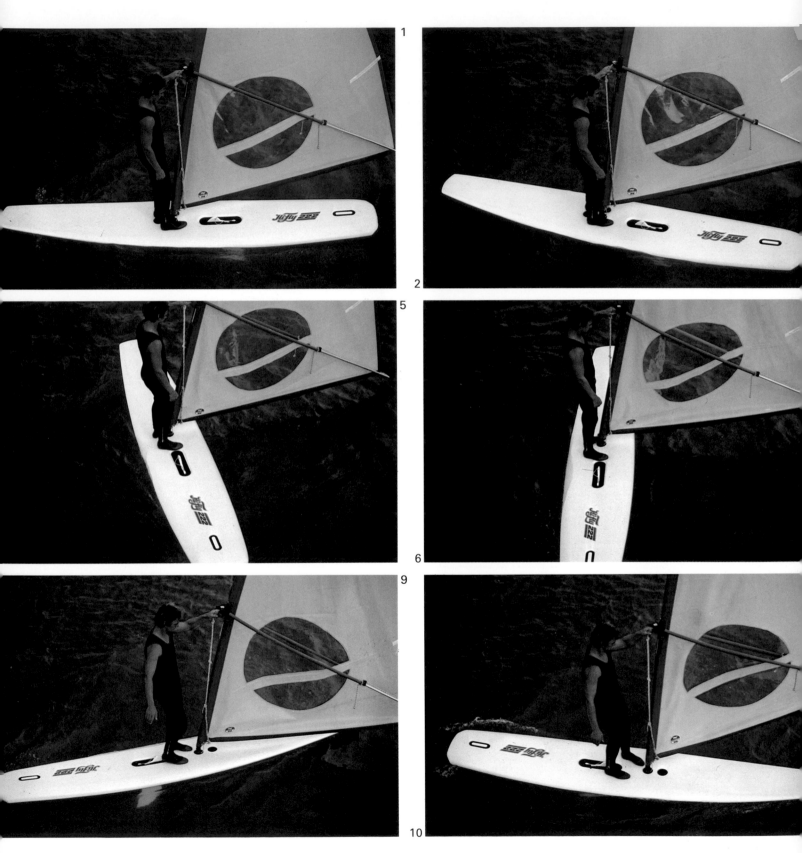

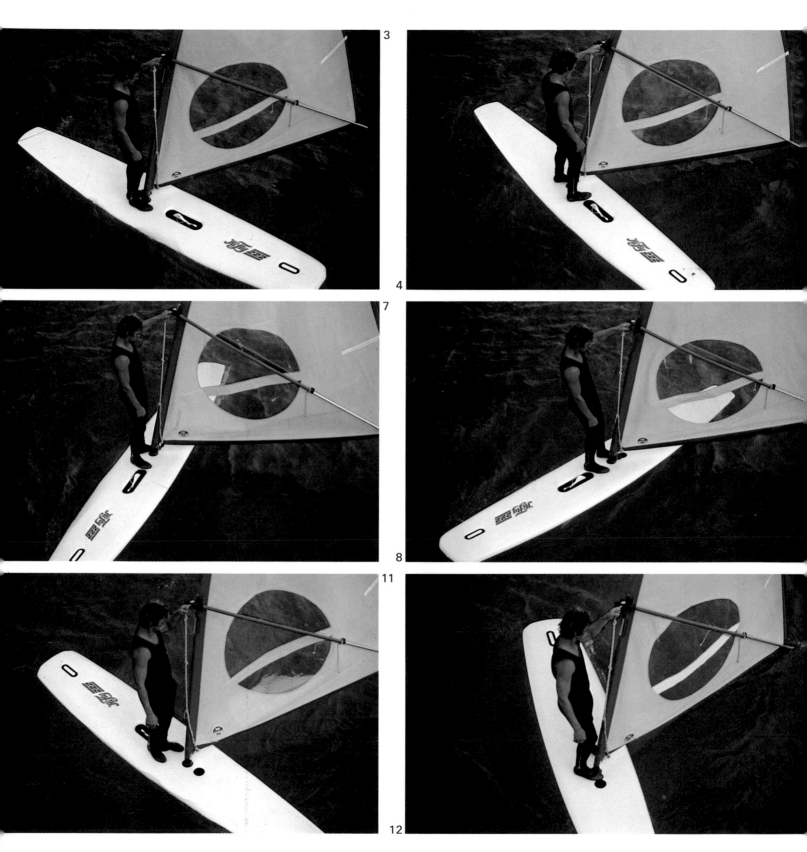

3

4

7

8

11

12

Hand positions

The most frequently used grip, the double-handed wrist grip with the thumbs pointing toward one another, also known as the overhand grip, follows naturally from the attachment of the boom being at shoulder height. This method is favoured by practic-ally all boardsailors because it puts the fingers on the rubber covering of the wishbone and thereby makes for a good solid grip. Pulling in and letting out the sail are easy to do, since the wrists are not flexed. In light to medium strength wind only the overhand grip is used, as a rule. In stronger winds one can relax the mast hand by changing to the underhand grip. However, the underhand grip with the sail hand is often found to be uncomfortable. The latter method — mast hand gripping from below, sail hand from above — is particularly suitable for broad reaching, as it makes pulling in the sail easier.

Holding on to the wishbone in a strong wind

requires enormous strength and endurance in the flexors of the fingers and wrists, as well as in the musculature of the arms and back. These muscles are strengthened by frequent sailing or through exercises, such as squeezing a tennis ball, opening and closing the fingers, flexing the wrists and arms while holding weights, as well as by doing pull-ups.

Important factors in making windsurfing less tiring are the thickness of the wishbone, what kind of outer covering it has and the size of one's hand. For example, a person with small hands should not use an excessively thick wishbone. At the present time, various types of wishbone sections are sold on the market — round, oval, six- and eight-sided. The most common are round and oval; the other two require a bit more getting used to. And no-one, beginner or expert, is spared blisters and callouses after an extended break, although leather sailing gloves can protect the hands until they toughen up, and keep off a chilly wind.

Starting

Take up the basic position, in which the board and sail are at right angles to one another. The sail is flapping freely, the feet are shoulder width apart, and the right hand holds the sail by the uphaul just below the wishbone and across from the front shoulder.

The left hand grips the wishbone, crossing over the right, and becomes the mast hand. It is about two hand widths (8 inches or 20 cm) away from the mast. Then release the uphaul. The mast hand pulls the sail to the centreline of the board with the help of a slight body rotation and by shifting the left foot forward. You should be looking towards the bow.

Now the right hand grabs the wishbone at a distance of 20—24 inches (50—60 cm) from the mast hand and becomes the sail hand, which slowly pulls the sail in. The boom should be approximately horizontal at this point and the board should be travelling straight ahead. The mast should be tilted to a greater or lesser degree to the front, if adjustment is necessary to sail in a straight line.

Surf sailing in Hawaii

After assuming the basic position, the start follows. The intention is to sail forwards in the direction in which the bow is pointing. The rear hand holds the rig by the uphaul. The position of the feet is checked: the front foot points slightly to the bow, the back foot is across the board's centreline — once again, check the angle between the board and sail and keep it at 90°. The front hand, which will become the mast hand, next grabs the wishbone about 8 inches

(20 cm) from the mast, thereby crossing over the back hand. Then the uphaul is released by what will now become the sail hand.

Important:

During and after the crossing-over of the hands the board should not rotate. If this occurs nevertheless, the mast hand can make a small adjustment by leaning the sail toward the wind. Simultaneously

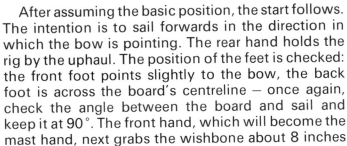

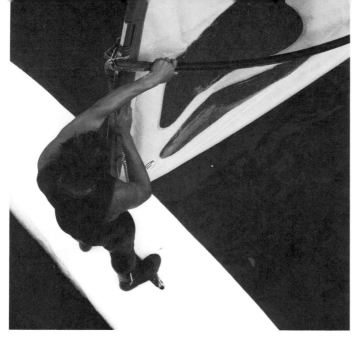

with a slight body rotation toward the direction of travel, the mast hand pulls the sail across the middle of the board. The rear hand, which is now the sail hand, grabs the wishbone at a distance of about 20 inches (50 cm) or shoulder width from the mast hand and starts pulling in slowly.

Counteracting the wind's force occurs simultaneously: the pressure is balanced by the body's strength and weight.

Should the sailor be pulled strongly to leeward by the sail, he can spill some air out of it by loosening up with the sail hand. In a light wind the strength of the arms is usually enough to hold the sail. In medium winds the body has to balance the pull of the sail by leaning backward, though at first one usually lacks the confidence to lean back. If the start was successful, the correct sail position then has to be found in order to sail in a straight line.

Starting

To recapitulate the basic position: the wind is coming from behind and the sail is at 90° to the board. The rear hand holds the uphaul just below the wishbone, across from the front shoulder.

The mast hand reaches over the sail hand, while the body remains upright. The mast hand grabs the wishbone as the sail hand releases the uphaul.

Pull the sail past the body. At the same time, the front foot is turned in the direction of travel and the sail hand then grabs the boom.

Sheet in the sail and balance the wind pressure. Never put an excessive load on one side of the board: it should always lie flat in the water.

Finally, the proper sail position has to be determined to keep moving forward on a straight course.

True and Apparent Wind Direction

One differentiates between three kinds of wind: the true atmospheric wind, the wind caused by the motion of the board, and the apparent wind, which results from the combination of the first two.

Every movement causes an exactly opposing wind, which is the wind caused by the board's motion. One should think of riding a bicycle in a complete calm: the faster one rides, the greater the wind so caused. In a breeze, as there is greater board speed, the greater this component of the apparent wind becomes.

True wind and the wind produced by the board's motion combine to produce the apparent wind, with

which it actually sails, as shown in the diagram on page 40 (left).

The apparent wind lies between the true wind and the wind produced by motion, except on a dead run. It always heads one more (comes more from straight ahead) than the true wind. The apparent wind in the range between beating and beam reaching is stronger than that of the true wind.

On a broad reach, the direction and strength of the wind one experiences are dependent to a considerable extent on board's speed. The faster one sails the more the apparent wind comes from ahead and the harder its force.

On a dead run before the wind, the direction of the true and the apparent wind do not differ. However, the strength of the true wind is lessened by the amount of wind caused by the board's motion: the faster the board goes, the less the apparent wind speed, if one is sailing away from the wind.

The sail's chord line

Steering is done by tilting the sail forward or aft, in line with the chord of the sail.

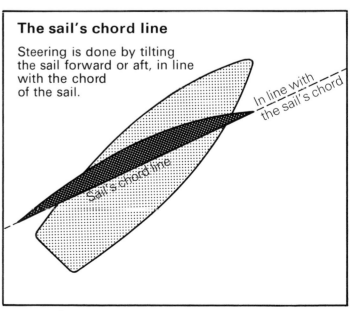

In line with the sail's chord

Sail's chord line

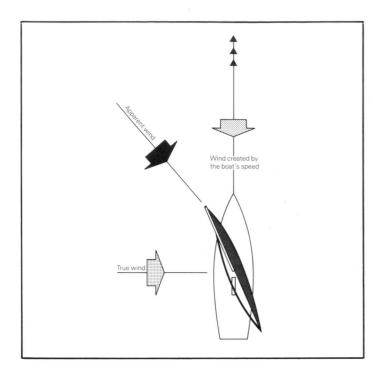

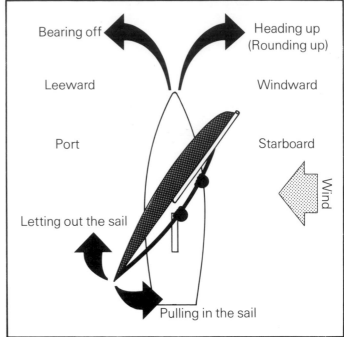

Steering

The sailboard is steered by the displacement of the sail's centre of effort (CE) from the longitudinal centreline. The centre of lateral resistance (CLR) of the board acts as a pivot in the water and the sail's CE as the point of action of the wind. Turning to leeward, i.e. heading away or 'bearing off' the wind, is accomplished by tilting the sail forward and at the same time pulling it in with the sail hand. This shifts the CE forward of the CLR and a torque is created which forces the front of the board to turn away from the wind.

This tilting movement, also called 'raking', should not be confused with any side-to-side tilting, or with the rotation of the sail around the mast ('sheeting-in' in boats) caused by pulling in or letting out the boom.

Heading up or 'luffing up', i.e. turning the board to windward, is done by tilting the sail back over the board's centreline. Thus the CE is brought behind the CLR and the stern is pushed round so that the bow points more into the wind.

These steering movements are carried out by the arms alone. The rig is displaced in line with the chord of the sail (page 39). The body position is not

changed as that may cause one to loose balance. By heading up and bearing off the wind, one can sail through an arc of about 135° to the right or left of the wind direction. This range is split up into different points of sailing. The beginner usually starts on a beam reach, with the wind blowing at right angles onto the side of the board (page 45).

Heading up more into the wind from a beam reach brings us onto first a close reach and then closehauled. The sail is pulled in until it is over the board's outer edge, and through zig-zagging, known as beating or tacking, to windward, one can reach a destination directly upwind which would be impossible to sail to directly. Sailing too close to the wind or 'pinching', however, cuts down the speed, pushes the board sideways downwind and requires a great deal of strength; really pinching will finally cause you to stop, as neither boats nor boards can sail directly into the wind.

By bearing off from a beam reach, one passes through a broad reach to a dead run, on which the sail is perpendicular to the board.

Every point of sailing requires the sail to be trimmed to the correct angle relative to the wind. The best sail trim is achieved when the luff, the area of sail next to the mast, just stops fluttering. This position can easily be found by pulling in and letting out gently with the sail hand.

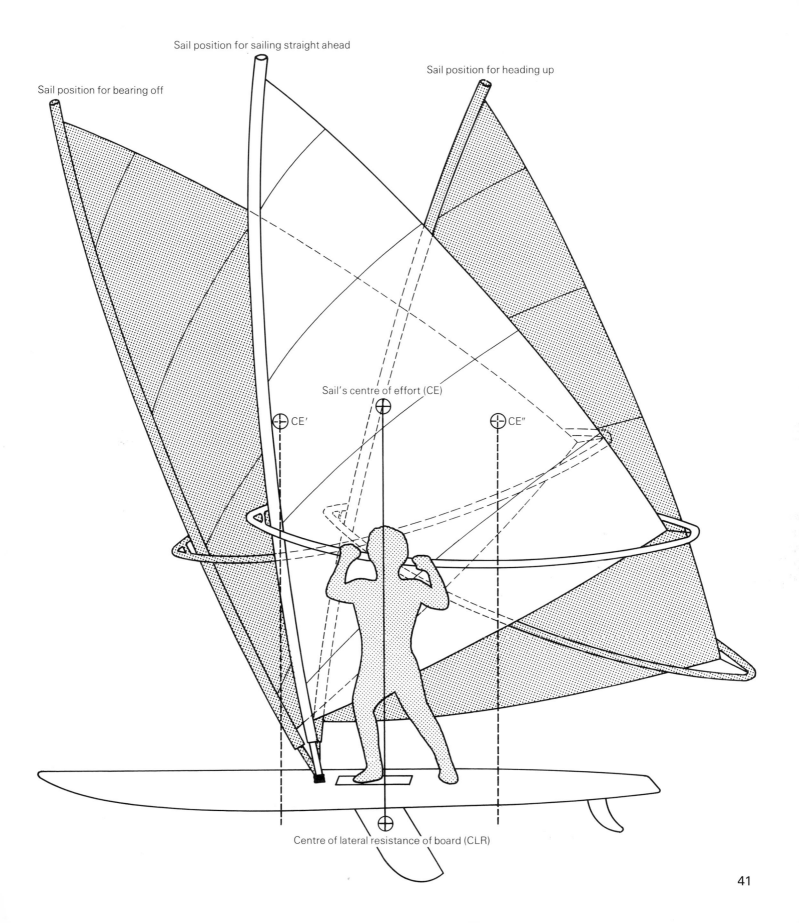

Sail position for sailing straight ahead

Sail position for heading up

Sail position for bearing off

Sail's centre of effort (CE)

CE'

CE''

Centre of lateral resistance of board (CLR)

41

Heading up (upper sequence)

In order to head up into the wind, the rig is raked back to bring the end of the wishbone down to the water, while the sail hand grips the boom farther forward, nearer the mast hand. The upper torso remains upright and only the arms hold the sail aft. The main pressure lies on the body's left side here, especially on the line through the left arm and foot.

The board turns more and more into the wind. Shifting the left foot back towards the stern helps, should the pressure on this foot from supporting the sail become too great.

Continue to head up until on the desired course. Then resume the normal balanced sailing position, meaning that the rig is brought back up and tilted as far forward as needed to sail straight ahead.

Bearing off (lower sequence)

Tilting the sail forward in line with the sail's chord, and the resulting change of direction to leeward, is called bearing off or falling off the wind.

The body remains upright, the front arm is extended, the rear arm pulls the sail in and thus is bent.

The pull on the sail previously directed to the side now shifts more to the front. The front foot, on the board's windward side and pointing slightly forward, must take this pull. The sail's CE lies far forward of the CLR and the board turns to leeward, or away from the wind.

When the desired heading has been reached, the sail is let out (freed) and the wishbone again held horizontal. In the last photo the sailor is beginning to head up again.

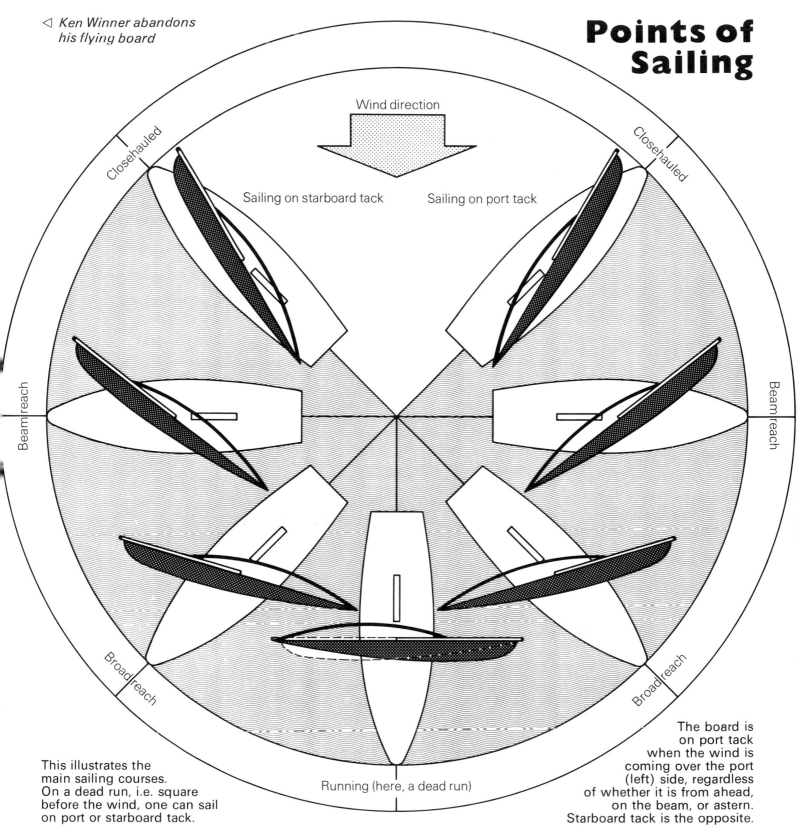

◁ *Ken Winner abandons his flying board*

Points of Sailing

Wind direction

Closehauled

Closehauled

Sailing on starboard tack

Sailing on port tack

Beam reach

Beam reach

Broad reach

Broad reach

Running (here, a dead run)

This illustrates the main sailing courses. On a dead run, i.e. square before the wind, one can sail on port or starboard tack.

The board is on port tack when the wind is coming over the port (left) side, regardless of whether it is from ahead, on the beam, or astern. Starboard tack is the opposite.

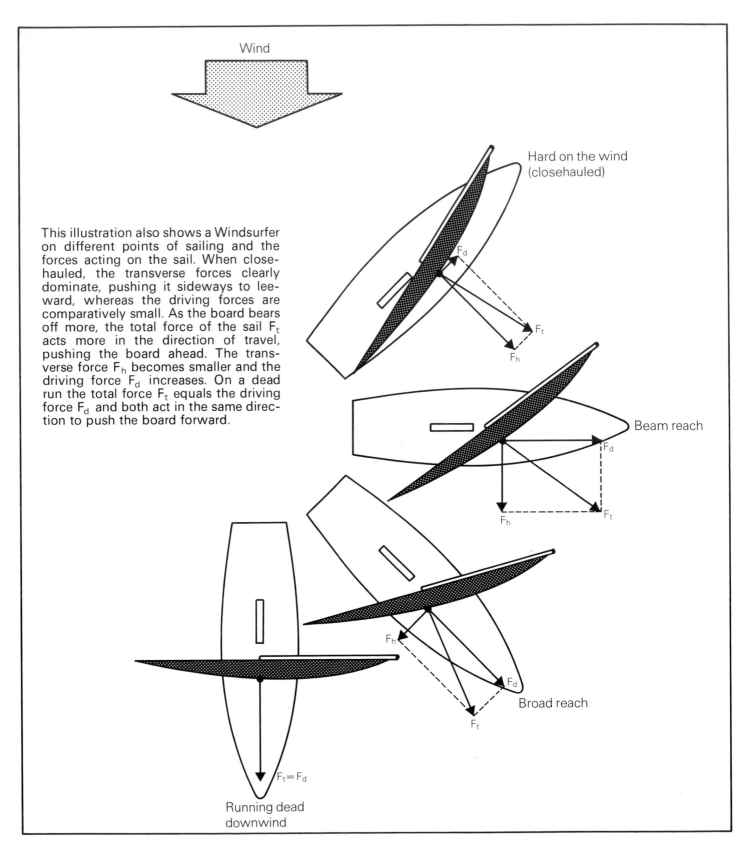

Wind

Hard on the wind
(closehauled)

This illustration also shows a Windsurfer on different points of sailing and the forces acting on the sail. When closehauled, the transverse forces clearly dominate, pushing it sideways to leeward, whereas the driving forces are comparatively small. As the board bears off more, the total force of the sail F_t acts more in the direction of travel, pushing the board ahead. The transverse force F_h becomes smaller and the driving force F_d increases. On a dead run the total force F_t equals the driving force F_d and both act in the same direction to push the board forward.

F_d

F_t

F_h

Beam reach

F_d

F_h

F_t

F_h

F_d

Broad reach

F_t

$F_t = F_d$

Running dead
downwind

Coming About

Coming about or tacking is a change of direction wherein the bow of the board or boat is turned into and through the wind, and the sailor and sail must change position from one side to the other, since the sail is always on the leeward side when sailing.

A tack is always initiated by heading up, regardless of what course one has been sailing on. The rig is tilted back until the end of the boom almost touches the water, as has been described. To speed up the turning of the board, pull the sail in over the stern to windward and remain in this position until the wind comes directly from ahead. This point is indicated by the sail, which begins to collapse and flutter (luff) near the mast. Then, the sail hand, after releasing the wishbone, grabs the uphaul. Step around the mast and complete the tack by leaning the sail against the wind until in the new basic position (see Rotating the board, above). After switching hands on the uphaul, a new start can be made.

A quicker version would be to initiate the manoeuvre as described until the sail collapses near the mast. At this instant the sail hand releases the wishbone and the sailor shifts from the normal sideways position to a transverse one in front of the mast. The sail hand, crossing over the old mast hand, grabs the new windward side of the wishbone and becomes the mast hand on the new tack. After positioning the feet for the new tack, the mast hand pulls the rig past the body and back to the front.

The crossing-over of the arms occurs only for a few seconds, since the old mast hand releases its grip immediately and grabs the wishbone on the new side. It has become the new sail hand, which carefully pulls in the sail.

It is important not to pull in the sail before one's feet are properly positioned on the new windward side.

A mistake at this point usually results in a swim.

Tacking to windward

Should a boardsailor find himself exactly downwind of his destination, he can still reach it by tacking to windward, sailing a zig-zag course close to the wind. A leg or board is the distance from one coming about (or tack) to the next, and one tries to gain as much distance *to windward* as possible on each leg.

Sailing such a course takes a lot of concentration as one must be able to adjust the board's heading and the position of the sail immediately, according to the wind shifts. This is done by bearing off if the wind heads you (comes more from ahead) and by heading up when it frees (comes more from the side). If you do not adjust the heading to the wind shifts, the board will slow down, or perhaps even luff up so much that it stops, or else you will not make progress to windward because you are sailing too far off the wind.

Coming about from starboard to port tack with a 'rope tack', begun by heading into the wind

The boom end almost touches the water's surface and the sail is pulled right in: wait until the board has turned farther into the wind.

Pulling the sail slightly in over the stern speeds up the turn. The sail hand releases the boom and grabs the uphaul. The sailor then moves in front of the mast. The mast hand releases the boom as the rotation of the board is continued by leaning the sail against the wind with the left hand until the new basic position is reached.

Grab the uphaul with the right hand and pull the mast past you. Begin sailing again by pulling in the boom.

Tacking with the crossing-over grip

It is possible to change direction faster by coming about with the crossing-over grip. A beginner can try this technique after a few hours' practice. The

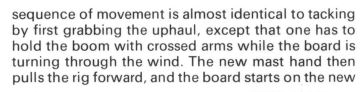

sequence of movement is almost identical to tacking by first grabbing the uphaul, except that one has to hold the boom with crossed arms while the board is turning through the wind. The new mast hand then pulls the rig forward, and the board starts on the new

upwind course. The sequence goes noticeably faster than with the basic technique. It is unnecessary to take up the basic starting position again and the sailor is able to sail on an upwind course immediately following such a tack.

This sequence presents a graphic demonstration of the crossing-over grip.

The switch is from starboard to port tack. It won't work without first heading up, so tilt the rig aft. The sail hand shifts its grip closer to the mast hand, allowing the body to remain upright. Rounding up is continued until the bow has turned through the wind. After the sail hand lets go, the sailor moves to be in front of the mast. The right hand (the old sail hand) then grabs the boom, crossing over the left, which then releases it. The new mast hand pulls the rig into the correct position simultaneously with the body's rotation. The sail hand (now the left in this case) is pulled in and the board begins moving on the new heading.

Action at Diamond Head, Hawaii (next page)

Running Before the Wind and Gybing

A prerequisite to gybing (turning the *stern* through the wind) a board is mastering the art of dead running. In order to get on this heading, one has to bear off until the wind comes squarely from behind. The direction of movement and the wind direction then coincide. While bearing off, one sails through a series of different headings and correspondingly the sail's centre of effort as well as the pull on the boom will vary.

It is important to pull the sail completely in, so that the wishbone is at the outer edge of the board, tilt the rig back, and wait until the board is heading almost in the direction of the wind. At this point, the body and the sail are turned about 45° – the sail is perpendicular to the board and the feet change from being on the windward side to a position on the right and left of the daggerboard. The important thing now is to keep the distribution of weight on the

1

2

board steady and even. This takes concentration because in its upright position the body can easily be caused to whip from side to side by a sudden pull on the sail or by waves. On a run, the board becomes very sensitive to lateral pressure. The stronger the wind the more this holds true, therefore you should venture out in a strong wind only when you have had enough experience.

(In some circumstances it may be safer to tack downwind with a series of broad reaches. If your gybing technique is not yet adequate for the conditions, you can even come about by sailing onto a reach, rounding up into the wind, tacking (the *bow* moving through the wind) and then falling off again onto a downwind heading. This is 'wearing round' and obviously far slower and less elegant than gybing; it is not illustrated here.)

Steering on a run is no longer accomplished by tilting the rig forward and back, but by displacing the sail's centre of effort to the left or right. The board turns to the right side if more sail area is present to the left of the centreline. It turns in the opposite direction if there is more sail area on the right side.

Bearing off onto a run

The starting position for this is the beam reach. The rig is raked forward in line with the sail's chord and pulled in by the sail hand, to push the bow away from the wind.

The direction of travel changes to leeward, and as the wind starts to blow more from behind one should get ready to rotate the body and the sail, along with changing the foot position.

The rig and one's body rotate at the same time, which is made possible by letting the boom out with the rear hand, to reduce the pressure on the sail. The rig and body rotation can only be carried out without difficulty if there is no large force pushing or pulling on the sail.

The sailboard is then running downwind. The sail is held upright (4). Running requires a great deal of concentration as the board becomes very sensitive to any uneven load on the edges, causing sudden changes in direction. Because of the sailor's position facing forward, gusts from behind or on the quarter are not noticed until very late.

Rope gybe (next pages)

In order to carry out this manoeuvre, the boardsailor must first bear off and head more downwind. The mast hand grabs the uphaul, and then the sail hand lets go of the boom.

The wind and the hand holding the uphaul pivot the sail over the bow to the new lee side. The other hand crosses over and grabs the boom and leans the rig to the front and gently to windward.

The new sail hand releases the uphaul, grabs the boom and thus completes the gybe.

3

4

1

2

5

6

3

4

Gybing with the crossing-over grip

The board is already sailing on a broad reach (1). By bearing off farther, the sailor gets onto a dead run with the sail out perpendicular to the centreline (2). The sail hand lets go to free the sail (3). The sail pivots over the bow to the new leeward side as the mast hand holds it up (4) by the wishbone.

The new mast hand grips across the other, and for an instant both hands are holding the rig in a crossing-over grip (5).

The new sail hand pulls the sail to windward and here the left hand becomes the new sail hand. The gybe is finished and the board is on the desired course (6).

Rope gybe (next pages)

The gybe is begun by bearing off as usual. The pressure of the sail becomes greater as the direction changes to leeward. When the wind comes from behind, the mast hand pulls the rig back to windward, while the sail hand lets the boom out. The pressure on the sail is at its least during this freeing-off and the body must be rotated and the feet shifted to straddle the daggerboard during this instant.

The sail is now across the board and its direction of travel.

The mast hand grips the uphaul — be careful as the board has become more sensitive to lateral pressure.

The sail hand releases the boom and the wind blows the sail over the bow to the new leeward side. In this case, the pivoting is guided by the left hand on the uphaul.

The new mast hand grips the boom, the sail hand releases the uphaul and brings the sail into the correct position to the wind.

1

2

5

6

3

4

7

Rope gybe, seen from above

The board is on a broad reach and continues to bear off (1). Gybing is simpler and quicker if one bears off even farther and overshoots a dead run (2, 3).

The mast hand grips the uphaul (4).

The sail hand releases the boom (5).

The sail is blown over the bow to the new leeward side by the wind, while the sailor helps it along by pulling sideways on the uphaul (5).

The old sail hand crosses over the hand with the uphaul to grip the boom on the new side and becomes the mast hand (6), and the other releases the uphaul and takes over control of the sail. The board continues to sail along on a broad reach (7) on the new gybe.

TECHNIQUE II

In medium and strong winds boardsailing requires more agility and energy compared to the almost static positions in light winds. Stronger sail pressure, higher speed, bigger and more forceful waves and using the body's weight to steer all interact together. These conditions place greater demands on one's sense of balance and agility of movement. Everyone has these capabilities: the movements and sequences need only be learned and practiced.

It is possible to boardsail in a more relaxed and tireless way with a dynamic body stance, in other words by taking advantage of the body's rotational momentum and using its weight effectively. The force transfer of the sail's pressure onto the board occurs mainly through the body, and the stance is a decisive factor in the speed achieved, as is shown by one-design racing. Of course other factors such as weight also play a role. Only through frequent practice does one find the correct foot position, the best place to grip the boom and the peculiarities of one's own board.

Launching from the Beach

This manoeuvre is only possible on a sandy or shingle beach.

After the sail is rigged and the safety line and mast pivot are fastened, the daggerboard is partially inserted in the slot and the board pointed into the waves. Next, the sail is pulled up by the uphaul, while standing on the windward side. The front hand (in this case, the right) grabs the rig at about eye level by the mast or the front end of the wishbone and the other hand holds the board's stern. Then the whole assembly is pushed into the water. Should the wind be blowing squarely onshore one must start off at a slant to the shore, closehauled to the wind. Winds coming from the side (on the beam) or from behind are more favourable. With a pivoting centreboard and only in calm water it is possible to bring the board to the water lying flat, as illustrated here. Boards without a pivoting centreboard are tilted as they are pushed out into the water, to protect the daggerboard and its slot. This latter method has to be

used in any case when there are higher waves. A board that is tilted to leeward is easier to push through the waves. Once in sufficient depth of water, let go of the stern and grab the wishbone with the sail hand.

At the same moment as you are climbing onto the board, you have to pull the sail in and push off from the bottom with the other leg. The wind pressure on the sail pulls you up onto the moving board.

When coming into the shore, sail at the minimum speed possible to avoid damaging the board. With those designs that have a conventional daggerboard in a slot one must remember to pull it up in time. The pivoting type of centreboard will rise up into the hull when it touches the bottom, although touching can cause abrasion or damage to the edges.

Shortly before reaching the shore, release the sail hand. Hold the mast with the mast hand and move to the stern of the board. Jump off when at the shore, lift the stern with the free hand and push the board in over the sand.

Take the tide into consideration, where there is any, and leave the board a safe distance back from the water, as it may otherwise be picked up by the waves and washed away.

The Theoretical Basis of Force Transfer and the Body Stance

by Hole Rössler

Body position in light wind

Body position in medium to strong wind

Observing a boardsailor, one recognizes that a remarkable number of forces act on him and the board, and that the movements which result are extremely complex and occur in three dimensions. In a technical analysis of windsurfing, one has to separate the unimportant from the important in order to be able to understand these movements.

Some of the forces which act on the combination of board-sailor-rig will first be studied. Let us consider the forces which produce drag, in the air and the water.

1. Form resistance of the board
   The underwater shape and the manner of the water flow around it determine this value. Displacement causes a small form resistance value for flat boards.

2. Frictional resistance
   This value is influenced by the smoothness of the surfaces around which the water flows, and the amount of surface area.

3. Induced resistance
   The fact that a sailboard does not always travel straight through the water, but is influenced by

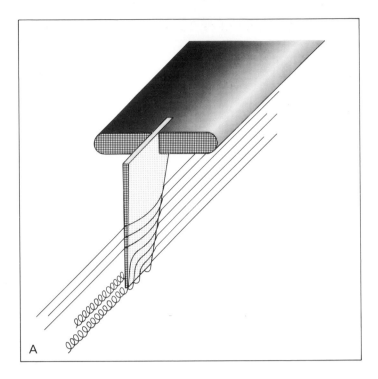

A

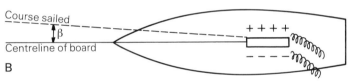

Course sailed

β

Centreline of board

B

force which represents the sum in direction and strength of all the forward drag forces. R acts in effect on the centre of lateral resistance (CLR), which is the centre of action of all hydrodynamic forces.

The hydrodynamic transverse or side force F_s, which prevents the board from sliding sideways due to lateral resistance, is another force acting on the CLR. The vector resultant of F_s and R is the total hydrodynamic force R_h. These then are the dragging forces on the board, as opposed to the driving forces, which can, under the right conditions, accelerate it to exhilarating speeds.

The driving forces are those which the kinetic energy of the wind exerts on the sail. A more detailed explanation of how these forces arise is given below in the section on the effect of wind pressure on the sail. For the technical analysis here, it is only important to combine all of the identifiable component forces, as was done with the resistance forces, into a total resultant force of the sail F_t, which in effect is exerted on the sail's centre of effort (CE).

The total aerodynamic force F_t is the diagonal of a parallelogram of forces, which is constructed from the positive driving force F_d and the transverse heeling force F_h.

When the resultant forces F_t and R_h are brought in line with one another, as in Fig. C, equilibrium is

the transverse force of the sail and thus moves forward with a certain amount of sideways drift (leeway), leads to differing pressure conditions on the daggerboard. These forces strive to equalize on its lower edge, which causes strong turbulance there. The more the sideways drift, the greater the eddies and thereby the induced resistance (Figs A, B).

4. Air resistance

A braking effect is caused by not only the wind resistance of the board, but also by that of the rig and the sailor. All of these forces depend primarily on the speed according to the following formula $R = C_w \frac{h}{2} A V^2$

C_w = coefficient of resistance
h = density of the medium
A = frontal surface area
V = velocity

One can think of the combined effect of all the underwater resistances (R) as equalling a composite

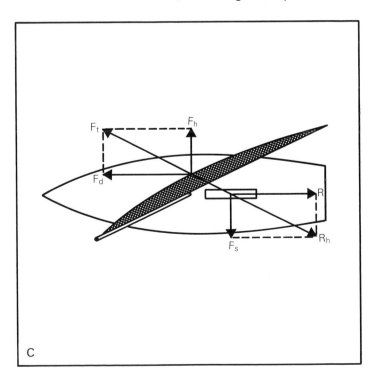

C

attained and the board travels in a straight line.

Looking at the board-sailor-rig unit from the front (Fig. D) one notices that the CE, through which the sail's total force F_t acts, is located above and to one side of the CLR, acted upon by the total hydrodynamic force R_h. This creates a tipping torque. This already represents the problem of balance, as well as that of the transfer of forces from the sail onto the board. On a conventional sailboat the wind forces are transferred through the fixed mast and standing rigging and tension between the sheet and the hull. The situation is totally different on a sailboard as the mast-board connection is flexible in all directions. The forces of pull, pressure and leverage all act on the 'sheet', which is the boardsailor himself.

The force transfer occurs through the sailor, who is the connecting link. The distribution of forces in conditions of equilibrium are shown in Fig. D. This illustration shows that the forces acting on the CE, that is F_{vert} and the vector resultant F_s, must be exactly balanced by those acting on the body's centre of gravity (BCG), i.e. the force of gravity G, the lateral component B_{lat}, and the resultant of these which is B_t or the tangential force.

· To make things simpler, we'll assume from now on that the board-sailor-rig unit is rigid, and in the following pages we will work for the most part with abstract illustrations.

While equilibrium has been attained in the lateral direction, those forces, or rather vectors, which transfer the sail's force onto the board and act on the CLR, are still missing from our description. They are depicted in Fig. E.

Since equilibrium exists between the sail's CE and the sailor's BCG, both must be acted on by forces which have the same strength in exactly opposite directions. Extending the end of every vector vertically downward to cross the lines of CE–CLR or BCG–CLR leads to the resulting vector P_{CLR}, which acts on the composite of all hydrostatic and hydrodynamic forces.

The board is acted upon by the vertical force of its buoyancy and the vector P_{CLR}, which acts at an angle to it, driving the board forward like a melon seed being squeezed out between the thumb and forefinger.

How can we determine the effects of the forces exerted through the BCG and CE? This can be done most simply using the formula for calculating the tipping moment:

Tipping moment M = force K × length of lever arm a
or　　　　　　　　M = force K × radius r × sin α

Looking more closely at the formula and its implications, one realizes why the body's weight is shifted outward in a strong wind. The angle of sin α is increased by leaning out farther, and thereby also the moment of the BCG, which can thus balance a greater tipping moment acting on the CE.

The rules of leverage help to answer the question of whether it helps if the boardsailor squats, thereby displacing his centre of gravity vertically downward. By squatting, one can increase the angle of sin α, but on the other hand the radius of the body's centre of gravity becomes shorter. Putting the values into the formula, one arrives at a reduction in the moment, and hence in the counteracting effort. Without any doubt, however, squatting does have one advantage, in steadying the boardsailor's stance.

Until now only the forces and vectors in the vertical plane have been discussed, whereas in reality those in the horizontal and oblique planes also have an effect. These result from the wind, which is constantly changing its direction and strength; the water, which creates waves, causing the board to roll, drift and slide; as well as the mast and sail materials, which are elastic and allow the CE to shift about, as for instance, with varying degrees of mast bend.

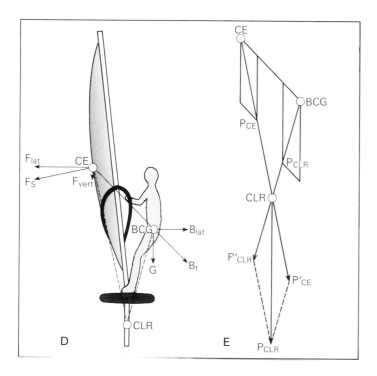

All these factors are able to cause, besides a vertical movement, a horizontal one. This leads to noticeable torques or turning moments which on the one hand affect the sailor and on the other the board, in that they rotate the board or upset the sailor's steady stance and make him fall. For these reasons one must constantly try to adjust to these forces, which are always changing in direction and strength. This may be done through a change in the surface of the board that is supporting it on the water by shifting the body's centre of gravity and/or by adjusting the sail's position.

A steady stance is determined by the following:

1. The tilt angle α, which is determined by the height of the body's centre of gravity and the horizontal distance of the BCG from the edge of the supporting surface. Thus a more stable stance is created by spreading the legs. This is very often necessary in gusty winds and choppy waves.

2. The height of the body's centre of gravity must be lifted and is likewise determined by the tilt angle. With an increasing angle α, the height it must be lifted also increases, and thus the work which must be done to bring the body out of equilibrium.

3. The dynamic stability. What is meant by this is that the body remains standing steadily as long as the force vector K, the resultant of the lateral force F_{lat} and gravity G, runs through the supporting surface. The resulting angle is not identical to the tilt angle α, since it is affected by F_{lat} and G, and has nothing to do with the position of the centre of gravity of the size of the supporting surface.

Shifting the BCG can be accomplished by bending or stretching one leg, taking steps sideways or backwards with both legs, and by a combination of these. The rig's position with respect to the board's transverse or horizontal axis can be altered by letting out or pulling in the sail. Of course, combinations of adjustments are also possible and the boardsailor has ultimately to decide what to do from situation to situation to maintain optimal performance and a secure stance.

Body stance

The basis of learning a number of sports, including windsurfing, is becoming able to carry out movements instinctively. Boardsailing instinctively means

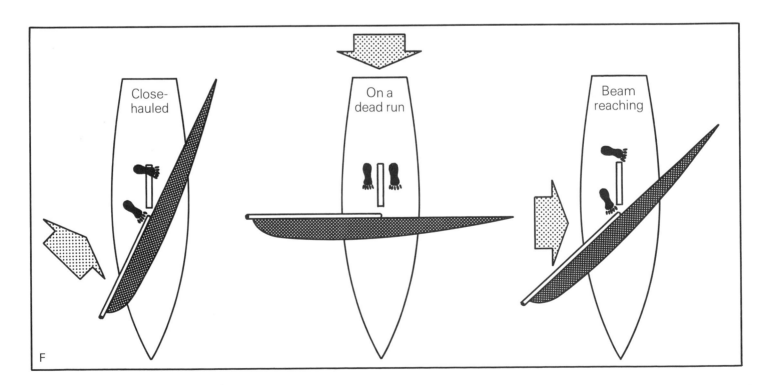

standing upright and relaxed, and being able to feel whether one has achieved the best body stance at an optimal angle to the board and sail. Using the body's weight and size for effective leverage makes sailing less tiring.

Discovering the proper body stance requires a lot of sensitivity and practice. Important factors include the surfer's body size, the form of the sail and board (whether a displacement or a planing type), as well as the distance between the vertical projection of the CE and the CLR (position of the mast step, daggerboard and skeg). Every point of sailing also requires special techniques, which again depend on the type of waves present. Ideal conditions to start in are a steady light wind, smooth water and a course which lies between a beam reach and closehauled. The centre of pull on the boom can be found by bringing the hands closer together until the pull is balanced. On a beating course in a medium to strong wind, the hands hold the wishbone at about 8 inches (20 cm) on either side of this point, with the front arm stretched and the rear arm slightly flexed.

One can try to minimize the air resistance of the body by slightly rotating the upper torso. The optimal stance results from the combination of the hands' grip on the wishbone, the position of the arms, and a slight upper body rotation.

You should never grip the wishbone with the hands too far apart or have both arms fully flexed. This quickly makes one tired and results in poor air flow around the body and rig.

Force transfer

The transfer of the wind's force onto the board occurs through the body and the feet. The feet should be placed as illustrated by Fig. F, in order to counteract the pull of the sail, which is diagonally to the front, except when running dead downwind.

An upright body stance (almost a straight line from head to feet) and the correct distance between the body and the sail make for higher speed and better endurance.

The Effect on Performance of the Distance between the Body and the Sail

The negative effect of the body on performance results from its wind resistance area and its influence on the air flow onto the sail. The body acts to diminish performance principally on points of sailing closer into the wind than a beam reach, because the resistance vector is working against the propulsion vector. This wind resistance of the body cannot be reduced, in contrast to the body's effect on the air flow onto the sail's windward side.

Areas of high and low pressure are produced when air flows past the body, which has an oval cross-section. This is unalterable, since no one can make himself smaller without affecting his centre of gravity and form. Furthermore, the air flow around the body

reduces that onto the sail's windward side. Instead of being drawn apart by the shape of the sail, and thus increasing the force, the flow lines are crowded together and stirred up by the body. The pressure on the sail's windward side decreases and it is noticeable that the sail isn't pulling as well. For these reasons, one has to try by all possible means to increase the distance between the body and the sail so as not to disturb the air flow onto the sail.

This is particularly true in lighter winds. In a medium wind, many racing sailors use a wishbone with a greater width in order to try to achieve more forward thrust through a more fully curved sail. A positive side effect of this is the increased distance

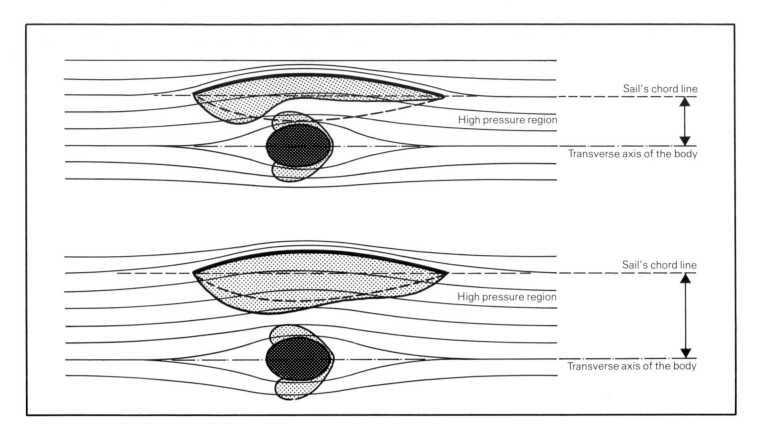

Sail's chord line

High pressure region

Transverse axis of the body

Sail's chord line

High pressure region

Transverse axis of the body

between one's body and the sail. However, one should sail with flexed arms when running or beam-reaching in medium winds, for the following reasons:

1. So that you do not stand too far aft. This would cause a poor position of the board in the water and have a braking effect.

2. Sudden gusts can be survived by letting out the sail. One has to work hard on these points of sailing in stronger winds and higher waves, pushing the sail in by using body rotation and pushing against the board with the front foot in order to catch up with the waves and plane with them. The fastest sailor on a closehauled course is the one who avoids frequent or large corrections of the sail trim or his body and foot position, and thus frequent direction changes and uneven loading on the board.

Bearing off and heading up in medium to strong winds

Bearing off

This series of photos shows the many influences on the sailor, board and rig that have to be taken into consideration. In order to avoid a catapult fall or the board tilting on edge, one has to be able to co-ordinate direction changes, increases in speed, force changes on the sail, increasing muscle tension and loading of the board.

The catapult fall is a phenomenon with which only boardsailors are familiar. Quite suddenly, one is literally snatched off his feet and catapulted into the water, often after flying in a high arc. The main reason for being hurled off and forward is a change in direction of the pulling force on the sail, which suddenly acts outside the area in which it is supported or balanced and reaches considerable proportions. Greater torques exist if the sail's CE is located outside the board's longitudinal axis, and in addition the centrifugal forces, which occur when sailing through an arc, are greater at higher speeds.

Initially, one is able to brace against these forces, but when sailing through an arc a strong forward pull develops which can only be balanced out by leaning the entire body weight farther back. If the pull is too strong and the sail is brought in too far, an otherwise avoidable catapult fall becomes inevitable. It can only be prevented by letting out the sail: bearing off is then interrupted and the entire procedure has to be started anew.

During the preparation phase, the grip on the boom should be shifted about 8 inches (20 cm) back. The front foot is turned slightly in the direction of travel and placed on the windward side next to the daggerboard, while the back foot is placed across the board's centreline behind the slot. At the same time the sail's CE is shifted and the boom pulled in, and the body's centre of gravity has to be brought down in order to brace oneself with enough weight and strength against the sail's pull. Too much pressure on the back foot makes the board tilt to leeward, and an imminent fall can only be avoided by letting the sail out and putting pressure on the windward side with the front foot.

Bearing off onto a run (upper series)

Bearing off begins with the mast hand gripping the boom somewhat farther back. The sail hand then pulls in, the mast is tilted forward in the direction of the sail's chord line and the body's centre of gravity is lowered. The front foot pushes against the board to turn it, if possible, when on a wave, while the back foot pulls the stern to windward.

The force on the sail shifts, and the forwards pull becomes very strong.

The board is held level while going over the wave. Wait for a favourable moment to change from the partially sideways stance to a position across the longitudinal axis of the board.

The body turns while one rapidly frees off the sail; the front foot is placed next to the daggerboard and the body straightens up.

Bearing off onto a run (lower series)

The normal sailing position is assumed first. The boom is then gripped somewhat farther back with the mast hand and finally the rig is tilted to the front as shown and pulled in decisively with the sail hand. The back foot helps the board rotate by pressing the back of it to windward; the pressure of the sail is now at its strongest. The board is made to turn faster by shifting the body's centre of gravity to the back and lowering it by bending the knees. Putting more weight on the windward edge also facilitates turning to leeward. The wind is coming in over the quarter so that the board is on a broad reach; one then prepares to turn the body.

The sail is let out and together with the rig the body is rotated to windward.

This, in conjunction with straightening the body and shifting the feet, can only be carried out while there is no wind pressure on the sail and the muscles are relaxed.

Robby Naish jumping a wave

Heading up or rounding up

Quick action and the confident performance of manoeuvres is often required by the sudden appearance of obstacles or by being obliged to yield to another board or boat. In contrast to bearing off, the course is changed to windward, in other words the board heads more into the wind. The speed decreases and the pull on the sail changes.

The initial position in this photo sequence is broad reaching while passing a wave.

The sailor moves to the back in order to tilt the rig aft and weight down the stern. The front foot is next to the daggerboard slot and is turned in the direction of travel, while the other is 12 to 28 inches (30–50 cm) farther back in the middle of the board. The body leans diagonally backward in order to counter the sail's pull; the feet transfer this force onto the board behind the CLR and the board turns. At the same time the length of the waterline decreases,

diminishing the board's resistance to being rotated and allowing it to head up more readily.

The closer the board sails into the wind the slower its speed becomes. The turn is continued as the arms keep the sail pulled in. The sail has to be held in more and more in heading up until one is almost angled into the wind, in order to keep from destroying the air flow on the leeward side. In the final phase shown here, the sail is pulled slightly too far across; the normal sequel to this would be to come about.

Tacking and Gybing with the Mast Hold Technique

Tacking with a mast hold (from right to left)

The most frequently used technique for coming about uses a mast hold. There are two possibilities: either the mast hand grabs the mast first or the sail hand does so.

Which method is used depends in part on how easily one's particular board turns. With a board that turns effortlessly through the wind, there is no need

to tilt the sail far to the front at the beginning of the new tack. On the other hand, many racing boards turn poorly; the change of sides is executed while the board points into the wind. These boards also need to bear off more strongly first, to get up speed, which is easier when using the second variant. Coming about sharply usually makes sailboards loose all momentum and is not a good practice.

Coming about from starboard to port tack: here the sail hand crosses over and grabs the mast.

Rounding up is begun from a closehauled course. The back leg is braced against the pressure on the after (left) side of the body. When the board has turned through the wind, the sail hand releases the boom. Look out: there is no sail pressure any more! The mast is then grasped below the boom. At the same time the right foot is placed in front of the mast, the rig is pulled by the mast past the body with the left arm, and one quickly changes sides on the board. The sail stands free for a few moments, then both hands grab the boom and pull it in.

1

2

5

6

3

4

Tacking with a mast hold

During the rounding-up phase, one must already have a good idea of the following sequence of movements. Every change of grip and foot position has to be executed well.

1. Luffing-up — the sail is pulled fully in, the left leg carries most of the body's weight and the sail pulls strongly to the side and back.

2. The speed diminishes and turning is accelerated by pulling in with the sail hand.

3. The mast hand (here the right) grabs the mast below the boom, while the sail hand pulls the sail across even farther. The board has already turned through the wind.

4. After releasing the boom, the sailor shifts around the front of the mast to the new windward side and the mast hand pulls the rig past the body to the new leeward side and tilts it forward.

5. The mast stands free for a moment, and both hands quickly grab the boom at the proper distance from the mast. The position of the feet still has to be adjusted a bit.

6. The tack has been completed and the board picks up speed as the sail is pulled in.

The tension and drama are obvious: Karl Messmer during a critical tack just before the finish. It brought him to victory and made him European Windsurfing Champion at Lake Garda in 1980.

5   4   3

Tacking with a mast hold (from right to left)

1, 2. Here it's very clearly seen how the body braces itself against the pulling force acting to the side and back. Correct foot position and a solid stance are required for the quick execution of this tack.

3. After releasing his sail hand, the sailor moves toward the board's bow: the sail hand then grabs the mast. At this moment there is no force on the sail. One nimbly changes sides by straightening the legs, in a way similar to the weight transfer in a stem christie in skiing.

2   1

4. The sail is tossed in a slight arc against the wind during its unsupported phase. The body rotation and change of side are completed at this time.
5. Both hands grip the boom and pull it in. The sail starts to pull and the body's weight counteracts this.

Next two pages: a fast tack from port to starboard is shown. Here the sail hand grabs the mast first (second photo from left). It is clear that the sailor is changing sides during the moment when no force is acting on him and the sail.

Tacking with a mast hold (from right to left)

The execution of a tack is dependent on the situation. An obstruction that suddenly appears often forces one to come about quickly and thereby lose momentum. The illustration here shows a drawn-out tack, which barely affects the speed. Changing sides is also done more slowly. Especially in light winds, valuable distance can be gained by coming about smoothly, sailing the board around.

The pictures also show the large turning radius of this kind of tack.

Coming about with a mast hold
(from right to left)

The perspective in the lower pictures clarifies the most important movements during this tack. The left picture in the sequence shows the sail being pulled in and over to the windward side. Note that not much speed has been lost.

With the sail hand on the mast, the left leg then pushes forward and one makes a quick foot transfer to turn around the mast.

The left hand then grabs the boom, the body rotation is completed, and the front hand releases the mast and quickly grabs the boom. The sail is pulled in forcefully and the board picks up speed.

Steering while running

In order to be able to sail straight ahead on a run there must be the same amount of sail surface on the left and the right sides. The feet are placed straddling and close beside the daggerboard, the body is relaxed and upright, and the knees are slightly bent in order to absorb wind and wave variations. The slightly bent arms, kept shoulder's width apart, hold out the wishbone to be able to react to sudden wind gusts.

As previously mentioned, sailboards react to side loading. By shifting one's weight to the left side a board is steered in an arc to the right, and by pressing on the right side it turns to the left. The length of the daggerboard is the cause of this. (For this reason, in wind strengths above Force 4-5 one either removes or pivots up the board.) Experienced sailors often use their weight to steer independently of the sail.

When the sail is tilted to port the board travels to starboard, and vice versa. If the CE is displaced to one side, the board turns in the opposite direction. Steering movements of the rig should be made carefully and sensitively to keep from being thrown off balance by a sudden and violent direction change, especially in stronger winds.

Gybing

The gybe, the most beautiful manoeuvre in wind-surfing, is a lot more fun to perform than coming about, for those who have mastered it. This type of direction change is something of a show when executed cleanly, even in only moderate winds. The brisk dynamic movements as well as the spinning of the sail are impressive to watch. There is no loss of speed in gybing; on the contrary, if done well, one can actually accelerate by quickly hauling in the boom.

Clean manoeuvres are particularly important in running at the turning marks for the broad reach and running legs. A good deal of distance, as well as the right-of-way advantage, can be gained. In a good gybe the movements are smoother and more fluid, speed is not diminished and the sailor does not need to change sides quickly or hectically.

Apart from a stop gybe, bearing off strongly always precedes a gybe. In the next chapter gybes from different points of sailing will be demonstrated.

Both of the following picture series illustrate the mast hold technique, in which either the mast hand or the sail hand can grab the mast first. Regardless of the course being sailed, bearing off onto a run is first necessary. In order to carry out the gybe more quickly, one bears off even farther than onto dead run, meaning that the bow points in the desired new direction while the sail remains in the old position. The mast hand grasps the boom about 28 inches (50 cm) behind the mast to shift the rig to windward; in addition, the turn is accelerated by its pulling strongly to windward and back. Then the foot position is changed, the boom is released by the sail hand and the sailor squats slightly. The sail hand next grabs the mast and pulls the fluttering sail aft against the wind. The rig is then spun gracefully around and, after straightening up the body, the boom is caught at the right moment.

Pulling the sail in and sailing off the wind is no problem. A buoy as a turning mark is useful in practicing, since one can then learn to decrease the radius of a gybe. Without a reference point the manoeuvre is inevitably carried out too slowly and covers too wide an arc.

Gybing with the mast hold technique

Both photo series depict a perfectly executed gybe using the mast hold technique, seen from different angles.

The upper series demonstrates an exaggerated squat, a method which is used particularly in high waves. The danger of falling is reduced by lowering the body's centre of gravity. This also makes the technique more reliable, and it is easier to bring the sail into the new position.

In these single pictures, one can see a tight turn made around a buoy as well as the grip on the mast. Unweighting the board by squatting makes it turn easily.

After the sail hand lets go, the movements must be carried out in synchronization with the board's rotation.

Gybing with the stern pressed down

Tense crowding usually results when a group of sailors in a race close in on a buoy all at the same time. Being able to carry out a manoeuvre in a narrow space requires practice. In these pictures one can clearly see how the sailor greatly decelerates the board by weighting down the stern. The sail pressure increases, the length of the waterline decreases by about a third, and the manoeuvre is carried out in a second. One usually has difficulty in carrying out the grip changes and shifting the feet so quickly. Also the end of the boom often hits the water and the wind blows into the sail from the front. The normal sailing position on the board has to be assumed immediately following the body rotation.

Gybing from a broad reach

A buoy serves as a reference point. In order to be able to turn through a tight arc, the sail has to be tilted far to windward and the leg on the outside of the turn carries more weight. In addition, the body weight has to be displaced more to the back in order to speed up bearing off and to make the board continue past a dead run. The sailor must brace himself

against the pull and the weight of the rig, which is tilted far back and sideways. The sail hand now releases the boom and reaches for the mast.

This manoeuvre requires sensitive and agile movements, for instance in bending the knees and rotating the upper torso, as shown here. That is the only way to make the necessary space on the board for turning the rig around. The new stance should be taken up before the sail is pulled in. Shifting the feet becomes more difficult in stronger winds.

Trapeze Sailing

by Karl Messmer

Trapeze technique

The early windsurfers had already began thinking about solving the problem of pain in the arms, a result of the relatively static loading of muscles and tendons when sailing in strong winds. The Charculla brothers introduced their so-called 'channel fitting' in 1974, which consisted of a wide leather belt with an attached line. A movable slider, which incorpor-ated a cam cleat, was fastened onto the boom on both port and starboard sides. The line on the belt was then wedged into the cam cleat. The sailor was thus suspended from one point on the boom, which could be moved by shifting the slider. Although this design noticeably relieved strain on the arms, it was never truly successful.

Trapeze knots

This knot is used to fasten the trapeze line onto the boom.

1. Tie a knot in the short end, which loops around the boom and over the long end of the line.

2. With the left hand, lay the short end over the long end.

3. Now bring the short end around the other and through itself.

4. The completed slip knot, not yet pulled tight.

The knot, while it is still loose, has the advantage that it is easily unfastened. It is loosened in a wink by pressing with the thumb. As a result, the trapeze line can be adjusted and retightened while sailing if necessary.

5

6

It took the Hawaiian sailors with their extensive experience of strong winds to finally develop the trapeze harness. They brought it along to the 1976 World Windsurfing Championships in the Bahamas. Some of those harnesses got to Europe and led to the discovery of a new dimension in boardsailing. Greater enjoyment and less pain from strained arms gave sailors a totally new and larger capability for using strong winds.

Boardsailing thereby became more elegant. The trapeze harness was a welcome aid for people who were prevented from sailing in winds greater than Force 4 because of their physiques.

The most widely used type of trapeze harness consists of a strong vest-like belt with a hook incorporated in the front side. A line, fastened onto the boom in such a way that it is allowed to sag in the middle, is placed in the hook when needed. This type of trapeze harness is sold in many variations. A few designs try to increase the wearer's comfort by evenly distributing the pressure on the back. Others pay more attention to safety considerations and incorporate buoyant materials to make it something of a buoyancy aid, or add a pouch for spare line, flares,

etc. In any case, when buying a harness one should be sure it has a safety release. After a catapulting fall one can be held under water with the hook tangled in the trapeze line. The only way to get free is often to undo the entire belt.

The two methods of attaching the hook each have advantages and disadvantages. When the hook is pointing downwards, hooking on is easier but unhooking becomes more difficult. One is relatively helpless against a sudden pull by the sail, as happens in a catapulting fall. If the boom is not too high this hook position can be used. When the hook points upwards, it does not allow for easy hooking on but it is easier to get out. This position is recommended for booms above shoulder height.

The trapeze line should be $\frac{1}{4}$ inch (5 mm) in diameter and 60 to 70 inches (150—180 cm) long, and is preferably fastened to the boom with an easily adjustable knot such as the one shown above. The line should hang at about elbow distance away from the boom.

The beginner using a trapeze should have a certain competence at his disposal and have mastered all the important manoeuvres in winds up to Force 3.

It is best to first practise hooking on and releasing with the rig on the shore. One quickly notices that a certain amount of momentum is necessary to catch the line with the hook, which points downwards. Next, this should be practised on the water in at least Force 2–3. A longer tacking stretch should be sailed while hooked on, however still without hanging with one's entire weight on the belt. Progress should not be made too soon nor weight transferred too much or the experiment will quickly end in a typical trapeze fall, because there is no longer direct contact with the sail and a sudden gust cannot be countered in time. The pull has to be equally balanced on the arms and the belt. The trapeze line should not be tied too short: the body should hang at about the distance from the boom that it would assume when sailing normally.

Boardsailing with a trapeze is similar to using a trapeze on a sailing boat, in that it is always done with an extended front leg. One should not unhook immediately if the sail loses some wind for a short time because of gust or a wave: try instead to keep the distance from the wishbone the same, even allowing the sail to flutter or be backwinded for a short while.

Running is seldom done with a trapeze because the sailor must constantly adjust his heading by moving the rig and thus would not have an even pull on the harness. Although the belt is a very useful relief on a broad reach, it demands more experience of the sailor than when beating.

The free-swinging trapeze line on the wishbone can easily catch the hook by itself and by reducing one's freedom of movement lead to a fall. To prevent this a strong rubber band can be fastened to the hook baseplate and pulled over the end of the hook when the trapeze is not being used.

Finally, it should be mentioned that a trapeze harness is not merely an accessory, endowing boardsailing with a greater sports potential by relieving muscle strain, but also represents an important piece of safety equipment. On the sea or large lake, suddenly rising offshore winds can cause problems for sailors who are far away from the shore. In such situations a trapeze has sometimes been a life saver.

Windsurfing in Breakers

Large breaking waves can make life difficult for an inexperienced boardsailor, not only in Hawaii, Australia, California or Mauritius but also on European coasts. One should not venture out in surf unless one can control the board in any wind strength and has enough local knowledge about the area, such as its currents, reefs and shallow areas. Equipment should include a high-wind daggerboard, trapeze harness, and in very strong winds a storm sail. Favourable conditions with respect to wind direction, wave height and shape, currents and tides should also prevail.

Just like conventional surfers do, the boardsailor should also observe the surf from the beach, in order to work out the wave pattern and to find a place where the waves break with less force, from which he can sail out.

If the sea bottom rises steeply, the waves break just before the beach and make launching very

difficult. If the start is unsuccessful one's equipment can be smashed to pieces by the force of the water. Over a gradually sloping bottom, where the waves begin to break far from the beach, launching is not difficult. A wind blowing parallel to the shore is particularly favourable.

After a successful start, the following should be remembered when sailing against breaking seas: never boardsail at full speed or with a tightly pulled-in sail into or through a breaking wave.

It is better to sail toward the wave at a good speed and then shift your weight to the stern to allow the

bow to climb over the wave more easily. If the wave breaks onto the board the sail has to be let out because the water slows the board and this makes the apparent wind come from farther aft. Usually the board is moved sideways somewhat as well, by the waves. One accelerates again by pulling the sail in

immediately, and usually has enough speed to take on the next wave. There are fewer problems with a light 'jumping board', with which one can surf or jump over waves which have broken or are just breaking.

On landing, one has to touch down gently and

with the stern first, otherwise the board may break from the sudden strain.

It is recommended, in strong winds above Force 4—5 and high waves, to either retract a pivoting centreboard or remove a daggerboard in order to avoid being surprised by a capsize. Some recent 'fun boards' make sailing in a lot of wind less problematic.

Should the board be caught by a wave from behind and lifted up and driven forward, try to accelerate by pushing with the legs. This means slightly bending the knees and at the same time pushing them forward. Speed can be increased by briskly pulling in the sail several times, and with luck one should be able to stay on the wave and surf with it. The wind caused by the speed becomes so strong at times that the sail is blown back against the sailor. One must then pull the sail in and change position accordingly. If the sailor finds himself in the wave trough and the board is losing speed, he should either head up or let the sail out and catch the next wave.

When surfing where wind and waves have the same direction, it's better to tack downwind, sailing diagonally down the waves and gybing frequently. The increased pressure in the sail helps to maintain balance. Also at higher speeds there are more frequent chances to surf down a wave.

If one wants to ride a wave back to the beach, it's best to surf diagonally down it and bear off sharply just before the shore to allow the wave to come exactly from behind.

To avoid submerging the bow, shift your weight to the stern. When the water becomes too shallow, jump off, grab the board's stern and push it onto the beach to avoid damage. As in launching from the beach, described earlier, the mast is held upright at the same time by the mast hand.

Wave-Jumping

by Karl Messmer

A particularly spectacular aspect of boardsailing is wave-jumping, which originated in Hawaii and has now become well known, primarily through the many photographs in sailing magazines. Anyone who has ever been to Hawaii and seen the beaches of Kailua and Diamond Head will tell you that wave-jumping could only have originated there. The constant, evenly blowing tradewinds and the regular surf of the Pacific Ocean, which rolls towards these beaches at close to a 90° angle to the wind, practically make it a necessary evil when sailing out to take to the air with the board. One sails full speed on a beam reach toward the oncoming wave and shoots up over the crest without even trying. Landing, however, does not always succeed so naturally, but we can at least fall back on the experience of the Hawaiians.

First of all, a few remarks are in order about the special equipment that is indispensable for jumping. Very little can be done in this surf without foot straps, double fins and a Hawaii style daggerboard.

The foot loops were developed by Larry Stanley and his friends, who very quickly discovered that although they were able to take off nicely with their standard boards, they then had no grip and ended up making rather uncomfortable dismounts. Apart from this, the boards became uncontrollable and flew unmanned through the air, imperiling swimmers and surfers. The foot loops brought an end to this problem.

The Hawaii daggerboard is shorter than a normal dagger and prevents a dreaded capsize. This simple and practical solution was arrived at quickly since boardsailing there is generally done in strong wind and tacking is seldom necessary. Later on, as special jumping boards began to be built, on which one was able to shoot through the surf on a board reach even better with a somewhat different technique, the manoeuvring capabilities were improved by the addition of more fins. Today the Hawaii daggerboard is sometimes replaced by a fin or even omitted altogether.

The specialty shops here are already carrying an extensive supply of so-called 'fun' or 'jumping' boards, which incorporate all of the improvements necessary for jumping. They have a flat bottom, a strongly bent-up bow, several possible fin positions, and a set-back daggerboard well when there is a board. The foot straps are custom fitted, and there are rigs with a special sail for strong wind and waves available for every type of mast pivot. In particular, the so-called Maui or fathead sail (Maui is the name of the island where it was first used) was made for surf conditions. The upper portion of the sail is enlarged to catch the wind over the waves better. The centre of effort is somewhat higher than usual as a result of the sail's special shape.

With equipment that is up with the latest developments real jumps can be performed even in moderate winds of only Force 4, and on small waves such as are found on inland lakes.

At high speed, one glides toward a small wave and presses the leeward edge into the water, allowing the wind to act on the board's underside and raise the bow up. On the wave crest, crouching somewhat helps in steering the board while in flight. The sail remains in the normal position or may be quickly pulled in for support. Experts have jumped up to 1 metre high and 3 metres in distance on the Gardasee using this technique.

Niko Stickl jumps at Diamond Head (next page)

Real surfing, however, can only be done on the ocean. Unfortunately, in Europe ideal locations for this are rare. The North Sea coast of Sylt, the Sardinian and Corsican north coasts, and the Biscay coast south of Bordeaux are all much-frequented surf areas.

How does one sail well in waves? One requirement, of course, is having mastered normal boardsailing, including handling strong winds. The equipment must be checked over and one should make sure, for safety's sake, that the mast pivot fits tightly in the board and that the rig is fastened with a stout line to the board. All lines should be tied securely and the sail size should reflect one's ability.

To stay oriented in the waves, one needs above all a good eye. The water has to be constantly watched: misjudgement in sailing into a breaker at the wrong moment can really get you into trouble. As a rule, remember that very regular waves always break in the same sequence, allowing one to seek out a wave in advance.

Surfing within the reach of a breaking wave can be dangerous, as one can easily be overtaken by the bubbly white water and be washed off the board.

Ideally, one broad-reaches up the wave and if there is enough speed lifts right off with the board. It's not a good idea to put too much pressure on the board with the feet, because there is a danger of pressing the bow to windward while in the air and thus flying sideways with no chance for recovery. So one should merely hang on the boom and hold the board with one's feet, in the straps, or at the most push it forward. When airborne the sail is slightly let out and lies parallel to the water's surface. Experts like Robby Naish stretch their legs after takeoff, press against the stern and thus momentarily turn practically upside down. The feet are then immediately drawn in again and the board is pulled into the landing position, which is almost horizontal with the tip slightly tilted up. While airborne, the sail acts partially as a parachute; it slows down the manoeuvre and makes it controllable. The Hawaiians graphically call the landing phrase 'parachuting down'.

Once the board touches the water, the greatest part of the impact is absorbed by the legs' elasticity. One should take special notice of this: many boards have been broken because the surfer landed with straightened legs and allowed his full weight to be taken by the lightweight jumping board.

Because of the tendency to head up in the air, caused by the normal foot pressure on the board, even experts often land slightly turned into the wind. To avoid falling, the feet are pulled all the way up and at the same time the sail is pushed out and backwinded a bit. This enables one to correct the board's direction quickly, following a somewhat oblique landing.

As spectacular as jumping is to watch, it really involves nothing more than mastering the basic technique. With some courage and by carefully observing experts, after a few attempts one can take off into the third dimension of windsurfing.

Sailing Rules
Code of Conduct

Every participant in watersports must act in such a manner as to not endanger, damage, hinder or trouble another, if possible under the circumstances. The basic requirement for this is a good knowledge of the right-of-way rules, which are part of the International Regulations for Preventing Collisions at Sea, called Collision Regulations or 'Col Regs' for short. These apply to all craft on the sea — ships, tugs, tows, power and sailing yachts, dinghies and row-boats, and also sailboards. They are not the same thing as the Yacht Racing Rules, although there are similarities in the right of way provisions. On inland waters, rivers or harbours there may be local byelaws or regulations which must also be complied with.

When racing, one may encounter other craft which are not: although they may go out of their way to avoid influencing those actually racing, they are not obliged to do so and indeed it may not be practicable. The Collision Regulations should be followed.

Similarly, although the principle that 'steam gives way to sail' is true, remember that pedestrians also have the right of way over motor vehicles, but still must behave prudently and reasonably. Power craft, whether yachts, fishing boats, ferries, ships or speed-boats, may also have constraints on the avoiding actions open to them, due to their draft, momentum, windage, manoeuvrability, minimum speed etc. Sailing yachts running downwind may find it difficult to gybe quickly, especially with spinnakers set.

Boardsailors should be aware that they may not be very visible to larger craft, and a board with its rig and sailor in the water is very hard indeed to see. A non-boardsailor finds it much harder to predict what a sailboard can and will do, compared to any other craft. Furthermore, beginners and racers are frequently so concerned with staying up and steering, apart from the fact that the sail blocks their view, that they tend not to keep the constant lookout in all directions that would allow encounters with other boards or boats to be considered and resolved with less haste and danger.

Right-of-Way Rules

Sailboards are on a par with sailing boats and have the same rights and obligations. The following rules apply for *all* sailing craft, whether boards, dinghies or large yachts.

When two boats are sailing with the wind coming from different sides and the danger of collision exists, the one with the wind coming over its starboard side (i.e. on the starboard tack or gybe) has the right of way: the other must yield. A simple rule of thumb is: wind from the right = right of way. If the wind comes from the same side for both craft, the leeward (downwind) one has the right of way: the windward vessel must keep clear. In either situation the craft concerned might be on crossing courses or meeting head-on. If a craft on port tack sees another to windward and cannot determine with certainty whether she has the wind on her port or starboard side (as on a dead run), the one on port must keep out of the way.

A vessel passing another, regardless of on which side, must stay clear and also not force the other to change course.

When a ship or yacht approaches that because of its size or for some other reason must travel in a channel, the boardsailor must proceed to the edge of the channel, or even go outside it, in good time, and may not hinder the other's passage.

The board is sailing to windward, while the dinghy is coming downwind, on a heading that will intersect the board's course and hinder it. Both have the wind coming over their starboard sides, but because the board is to leeward the dinghy is required to yield the right of way. Here it has luffed up, but it could also have turned the other way, perhaps gybing, and passed behind the board.

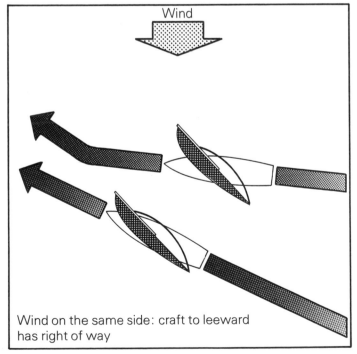

Wind on the same side: craft to leeward has right of way

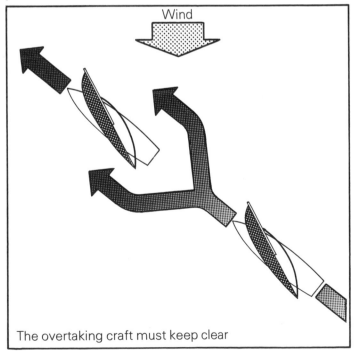

The overtaking craft must keep clear

A sailing dinghy and a sailboard are on a collision course (right). Since the dinghy has the right of way (wind from starboard side), the board must yield in such a way that it is obvious, and in good time. He does this with a stop gybe, that is by pushing the sail out against the wind, and turns away from his course to pass behind the dinghy.

Code of Conduct

To avoid unnecessary aggravation and possibly even a rescue mission as a result of plain carelessness, the necessary preparations should be made before every boardsailing outing. When choosing an area to sail in, one is usually confronted with the question 'Is boardsailing allowed here?' Prohibited areas are often marked with signs, although these can be easily overlooked. Generally, one may never boardsail in the docking areas, channels and shipping lanes for commercial vessels, or in the directional traffic separation lanes at sea. Should one, however, somehow find oneself in such an area, one must leave it in good time at the approach of a ship and proceed to the edge of the channel, or outside it: after all the depth of water required by a board is very little and one can go right into the shallows.

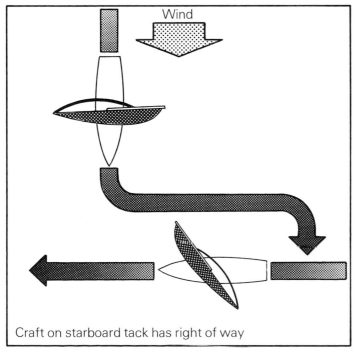

Craft on starboard tack has right of way

Nature preservation areas such as fish spawning grounds or bird nesting places in the reeds are prohibited, as well as landing on such protected shores or islands, and may be punished with a fine. Drinking water reservoirs will usually be closed to boards, if not to all boats. Novices and show-off boardsailors belong as little on a crowded beach as an elephant in a porcelain shop. The consequences of an accident are then usually directed against all boardsailors.

Once the right place has been found, information should be obtained about any unusual local features such as currents, tiderips, strong or gusty winds, wind shifts during the course of the day, etc. A number of sailors have been washed out onto the open sea by the ebbing tide or by tiderips and had to be rescued, sometimes even by helicopter.

Storm warnings are given differently from region to region. These visual or sound signals (flags, cones, lights or sirens) should be strictly followed, and it is worth getting into the habit of listening to the coastal and shipping forecasts broadcast for larger vessels. In the event of a storm warning, one should sail to shore immediately by the shortest route possible. As hungry for wind as one might be, and for strong wind, sailing out before an approaching gale can put one's life in danger. Surviving lightning or hail out on the water would also certainly keep one's guardian angel busy.

Boardsailing is generally prohibited everywhere at night, since the boards cannot be properly lit or seen.

As to equipment, depending on the prevailing weather conditions and one's ability, one should wear insulating clothing (wetsuit) and surfing or sailing shoes for a good grip and protection against injuries on any sharp edges on the board, a rocky bottom, sea urchins, etc. The frequent falls made by beginners can quickly lead to fatigue and hypo-

thermia. If one wants to do without a wetsuit, the air temperature should be at least 85 °F (30 °C) and the water temperature around 75 °F (24 °C); nevertheless, the outing should still not last too long because the effects of chilling can manifest themselves quite suddenly, and may make getting back difficult.

The lines and the knots on the inhaul and outhaul should be checked before every trip. For safety, an extra piece of rope (usable, for example, as a replacement inhaul, outhaul or tow line) and a loud whistle or a visible signalling device such as a smoke flare should be taken along. In an emergency never leave the board, since it is unsinkable and a good rescue device in itself, and easier to see in the water than a person. Give the emergency signal (repeated crossing of the arms over the head) and blow the whistle. Should you be out of hearing or seeing distance, only the friend or acquaintance ashore who was previously informed of your plans can help: you should make it a rule to let someone know where you are sailing, how far, and the anticipated time of return.

How does one get into such a dangerous situation? It usually occurs through over-estimating one's ability and physical stamina. A trapeze should always be taken along on longer trips and used when one's strength begins to fade, if not before; and extra clothing such as a lightweight wind and waterproof anorak or overall can be taken on the board or in a knapsack on the trapeze harness vest.

Very often the effects of an offshore wind are underestimated, since it seems relatively harmless near the shore. But it's difficult to see whether it is really blowing farther out, or how hard.

Another reason may be equipment failure, for example a break in the mast or boom, a broken universal joint, a torn sail sleeve etc. If you are unable to get back to the shore by sailing or with a temporary repair, the decision to take the rig down and paddle back should be made early enough. Unrigging far from shore is more difficult because of the stronger wind and higher waves, and paddling back takes a lot more strength and time, during which the wind and stream may become less favourable.

It's better to adapt a diver's rule to windsurfing: 'Never boardsail alone.' First of all, sailing is more fun with two or in a group, because of the shared experience; more important, however, is the fact that one is not alone in the case of a mishap or fatigue and can be helped through towing, replacement gear, or just good advice and reassurance.

Windsurfing and the Basic Physical Characteristics of Strength, Speed and Endurance

Strength

The beginning sailor in light breezes does not need a particularly high level of strength, since the rig stands on the board and only has to be held upright. This becomes a different matter once the transition to advanced boardsailing has been made, and winds of Force 3 or more have to be mastered. The force generated by the wind on the sail increases to the point that the sailor has to lean backwards with his entire weight in order to counterbalance it. And the higher the wind's speed becomes, the farther he must lean back. Waves begin to come into the picture in stronger breezes, making balancing and manoeuvres more demanding.

With increasing wind force the demands placed on physical strength, and especially on endurance, become greater. In this sport, endurance particularly means the ability to maintain muscle tension with a static load over a long period of time, for example as in beating in a strong wind, whereas in other sports endurance refers to maintaining movement and force over a period of time.

In moderate winds the muscles are still well supplied with blood since they are not contracted very strongly. But in a strong wind up to 60 per cent of the fibres of a muscle can be contracted, and because they thicken in shortening then can partially compress the capillaries. This results in decreased blood circulation and the accumulation of lactic acid in the muscle, which eventually becomes acidic and stops functioning. It is important to learn to recognize when this is beginning to happen.

When the proper training has caused an adaptation process to take place in the body, it can break down and buffer the products of metabolism for a much longer time. This explains the unbelievable endurance of the experts, who romp about for hours in the waves in a strong wind without showing signs of fatigue.

Speed

The expression 'speed of movement' implies the speed with which the body or parts of it are moved coupled with the reaction time and the precision of execution of the movements. The requirements for speed are dynamic strength, flexibility, elasticity and relaxing ability of the muscles, the neural and biochemical processes, and not to be forgotten, agility and will power.

Speed appears in boardsailing in the form of an acyclic quickness of action, or in other words, the speed with which movements are carried out to which there is little resistance, and which are not cyclic. An example is the manoeuvre of coming about, where one must change sides as quickly as possible around the mast to the new windward side. This particular quickness is developed through frequent execution of the necessary movements at different speeds, but primarily quickly once the correct sequence has been learned.

Endurance

The term 'endurance' denotes the ability to resist fatigue for a long period of time during physical stress. This does not come naturally, but is developed by the physical training particular to each given sport. Good function of the cardiac, circulatory, respiratory, neural and metabolic systems are necessary for good endurance.

Among the different types of endurance, boardsailing develops and requires above all strength and long-term endurance. Strength endurance means the ability to continue to apply a high degree of force over a period of time, and arises in heavy weather sailing in particular.

Long-term endurance can be defined as the ability to sustain uninterrupted exertion lasting at least eight minutes. The body's energy is produced almost exclusively aerobically, meaning that oxygen taken in from the air is oxidized in the process; usually there is a balance between supply and consumption. This type of endurance is limited only by the reduction of the glycogen reserves of the muscles. When they have been used up, one is unable to move any longer. It's important for this reason to take along carbohydrates in the form of sugar on a long outing, and remember that both trying to keep warm as well as exertion deplete the body's reserves.

The body's endurance can be increased by frequent sailing with outings of increasing duration and strenuousness as one's technique and strength develop. However, it is vital that one does not underestimate the tiring effects of this form of sailing, and of wind chill and even water that doesn't seem very cold; or leave oneself with too little physical reserve to get back safely if conditions worsen. Fitness training on land is possible all year around and can be adapted to the requirements of boardsailing, without the problems of climate, bad weather or safety on the water.

Windsurfing and Motor Equilibrium

A good deal of our everyday activity is dependent directly on the ability to maintain balance. Although we are seldom conscious of it, walking, standing or bicycle riding would all be impossible without a sense of balance. This has an even greater significance in sports where complicated movements are often done on the narrowest of surfaces, for example gymnastics on a balance beam, or in skiing, riding, rowing, skating etc. The exact steering of the body, board and rig in the flight phase of a wave jump is also a perfect example.

By the concept of equilibrium, one generally means the ability to influence one's own body or a separate object, when they are not in a stable state of balance, by such equalizing movements that they do not remain in their labile position. The ability to maintain equilibrium becomes apparent with the quick and most efficient execution of movement. The slightest threat to balance activates motor reflexes, which for the most part are carried out involuntarily and without our being consciously aware of them.

Generally, the motor sense of balance is divided into static balance or the ability to maintain a particular posture, dynamic balance or the ability to maintain balance during movement, and object balance or the ability to keep an object that is not part of the body balanced.

The biological basis of maintaining equilibrium

As stressed above, maintaining balance is a continually reactive process, meaning that the perception of the body's position in space is necessary at all times.

How does one register a change in position? The brain receives some information from the vestibular apparatus in the inner ear. The receptors located in the semi-circular canals perceive angular acceleration (rotation) while the receptors in the utricle and the saccule (located in the inner ear) perceive changes in the head's position and progressive acceleration. These give rise to involuntary reflex balancing movements.

Positional changes can also be registered through the eyes. One can also become aware through tactile stimulus (push-pull) of what is affecting one and one's surroundings.

All information is processed in the brain and leads to corrective movements via a reflex arc. These act primarily on the joints near the supporting surface. Every boardsailor can confirm this, since in leaning out the body remains straight as usual and only the ankle joint is extended.

The role of static equilibrium decreases with increasing wind strength: the board moves faster and the sense of dynamic equilibrium predominates. The consequences of one's alternations of board and rig trim are liable to be faster and more powerful at speeds, so mistakes are less easily corrected.

Wind and waves place high demands on the ability to balance and require great exertion from the body and the extremities to maintain equilibrium. The movements necessary to maintain balance are, of course, limited on a narrow board, particularly because of the arms and hands being fixed by their particular job of holding the rig. Despite this limitation of arm movement, the rig nevertheless represents for the beginner as well as advanced sailor an excellent aid for keeping balance.

A totally different method of movement, though, is required for it to serve as a 'balancing pole'. Higher pressure on a sail because of a gust is carried over onto the arms by the rig. This pull creates a stretching stimulus in the musculature which has to be answered with more aggressiveness. At the same time the lateral pull is the impetus which causes one to lean back more. Too much pull to the front is equalized by letting the sail out, while too much lateral pull is countered by letting go of the boom with the sail hand.

Finally, the size and relative position of the supporting surface of the board in the water can be varied by shifting the legs in certain situations. However, these movements are also limited because a step away from the centreline can easily tip the board, or cause it to dig in.

The Windsurfing Sail from a Theoretical Point of View

by Michael Nissen

Aerodynamics

Everyone who starts sailing will easily understand how one can sail with the wind coming from behind. The wind not only blows umbrellas and leaves around, but also boats. The sail acts as a pure resistance in this case, without the effect of an air stream along it, although there is some flow around the edges (A).

When running downwind the sail's cross-section is irrelevant. The only important thing is the size of the sail, the board's shape and the total weight. It is difficult, though, to understand how a sailboard is able to move forward with the wind coming from the side, or to even sail against the wind. In such cases the wind flows past the sail and a number of aerodynamic laws come into effect.

In Fig. B one can see a cross-section of a sail set at a slight angle to the wind, with the adjacent air flow. A part of the air current takes the long route along the convex side behind the sail, while the other part goes by the short concave route in front of it. According to Bernoulli's Law, the product of the pressure and the speed of a fluid medium such as air must always remain constant. Thus the faster leeside air stream is at a lower pressure than the slower windward one. The increase in kinetic

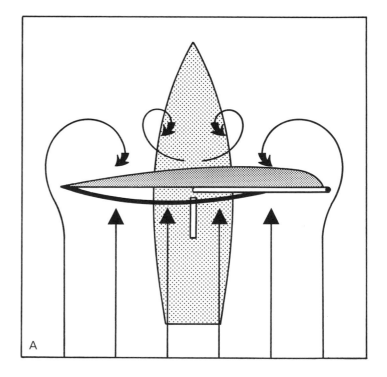

A

energy of the air movement happens at the cost of the potential energy of the static air pressure. These pressure differences can be proved experimentally with manometers: the faster the air speed on the

127

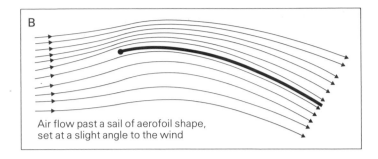

Air flow past a sail of aerofoil shape,
set at a slight angle to the wind

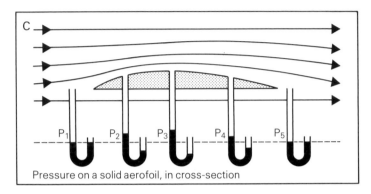

C

P_1 P_2 P_3 P_4 P_5

Pressure on a solid aerofoil, in cross-section

Air flow

Wind

α

CE

Perpendicular to the wind

Total force

Perpendicular to sail's chord line

Low pressure region

High pressure region

Sail's chord line

D

sail's leeward side becomes, the less the pressure there.

Fig. C shows an experimental set-up. An aerodynamic foil is placed in a wind tunnel. Several manometers (P) show, through the differing column heights of the liquid, that the lower pressure at different points on the convex upper surface of the airfoil varies. P_1 shows the wind's normal pressure before reaching the leading edge of the aerofoil. P_2 and P_3 show a definite decrease in air pressure, which becomes stronger at P_4. P_5 shows the normal pressure again without any influence by the aerofoil. A schematic diagram of the pressure distribution on a sail can be made from an analysis of the pressure decrease on the convex leeward side and the pressure increase on the concave windward side.

Pressure distribution

It is obvious from Fig. D that the amount of pressure decrease on the leeward side is much larger than that of the pressure increase on the windward side. The point of this, for every sailor, is that it makes it clear that the much greater forces occur on the sail's leeward side. He must therefore direct all of his attention to maximizing the leeward air flow and

strive to find the optimal position (trim) of the sail relative to the wind, and in particular to make sure that the leeward air stream is not interfered with. The mast causes a reduction of force on the sail not only through its own wind resistance but also by influencing the air flow, so that the pressure decrease on the foremost portion of the sail is somewhat reduced. A mast that is as thin as possible is recommended for the optimal efficiency of the sail.

Sail shape

If one compares a curved sail and a flat surface, it's easy to recognize that the curved sail produces more forward thrust. The secret of the increased propulsion must then lie in the curvature.

Which cross-section is best for sailboard sails? A rough method for determining cross-sections, which originated in the USA, is shown in E, which is a view of a sailboard sail, on which the cross-sectional lines have been drawn along the seams. The depth of the curve at the deepest point of the sail and the position of this point from the front is expressed as a percentage of the length of the sail's chord at each particular place. A sail's shape can at least be roughly estimated by these values. The actual shape of the curves across the sail, however, are not described.

Up to a point, the fuller a sail is, the more total force it produces. However, this total force vector points less and less to the front, and from the parallelogram of forces only a disproportionately small increase in the forward thrust force F_d results, while the heeling force F_h increases. In light winds such full sails are very fast. But there is a disadvantage to having such a full sail and thereby also a lot of curvature near the leech. The distribution of pressure diagram (D) shows that the lee side suction is perpendicular to the surface, and therefore the back part of the sail is producing a braking effect. Thus, strongly curved (full) sails are always very slow. Aside from this, the increased total force of a deeply curved sail must be transferred by the sailor onto his board. Even a strong person will only succeed in doing this in light to medium winds, since in strong wind the force of the sail will become too great, and he will also have to expend energy in counteracting the heeling force F_h. In choosing the curvature of a sail, one must take into account the different wind speeds that are expected and achieve a compromise.

The profile study (E) shows a sailboard sail in a Force 2 breeze. The belly or camber lies relatively far forward due to the low tension on it, and the curve tapers off to practically a straight line at the leech.

A good cross-section for a sail is a fullness of 13 to 15 per cent in light wind at a position between 43 to 45 per cent of the chord length measured from the front. In strong wind the camber should not go back farther than 45 per cent and its depth should come to about 10 per cent. If the sail's front portion is too full and the belly lies too far forward, say at 40 per cent, the sail will be considerably less close-winded (able to point high into the wind). A sail with its camber lying more than 55 per cent of the chord length to the back, will suffer the braking effect of the closed leech, described above.

For the vertical cross-section distribution, one can say that the camber should be relative to the respective chord lengths in approximately the same place throughout the entire height of the sail. The depth of the sail should increase from the bottom upwards and not start becoming flatter until the head. A good vertical distribution of fullness for a boardsail would be a cross-section depth at about the boom height of 12 per cent, then increasing to 14 per cent until

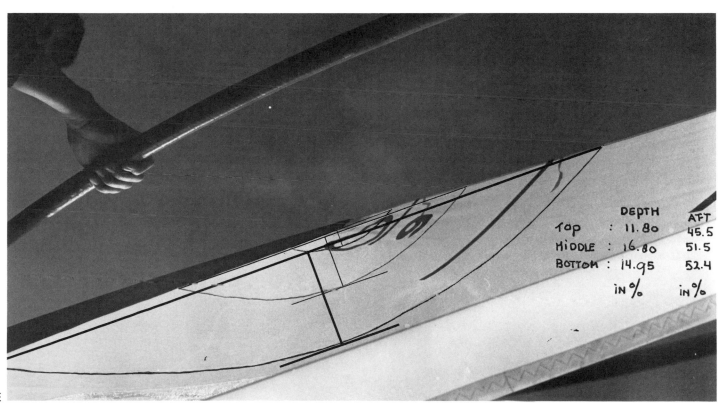

E

DEPTH   AFT
Top   : 11.80   45.5
MIDDLE : 16.80   51.5
BOTTOM : 14.95   52.4
        in %   in %

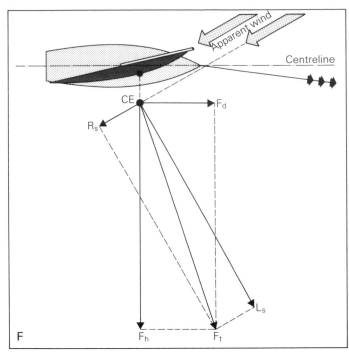

the head, where it again returns to 13 per cent of the length of the horizontal chord.

One really ought to look up at or photograph the rigged sail from below, as in E, and measure once the camber depth and position, in order to get an idea of the sail's shape. This can be done with an upright or horizontal test rig on land.

These statements are of course only approximations and sail makers don't really like to let anyone in on their secrets. Nevertheless, they are enough to help one sift the wheat from the chaff.

Forces on the sail and board

The wind that strikes the sail is slowed by the mast and sail itself, the body of the sailor, and even the board, and thereby causes resistance or drag, which is comparable to that of the air opposing the motion of a car or a bicyclist. This air resistance R_s is relatively small in the case of the sail. The previously

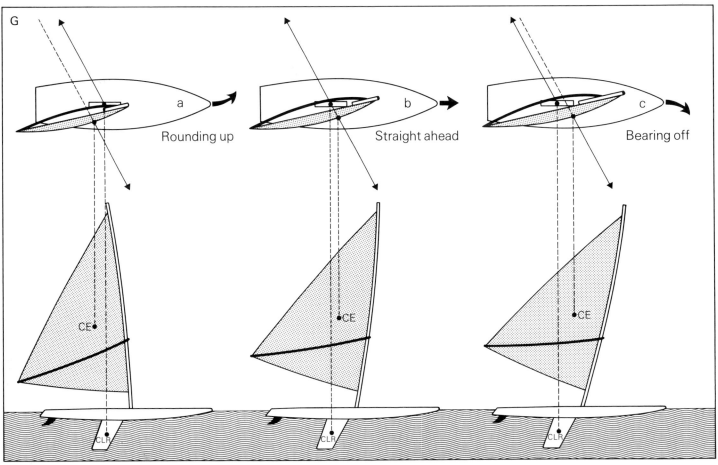

a Rounding up

b Straight ahead

c Bearing off

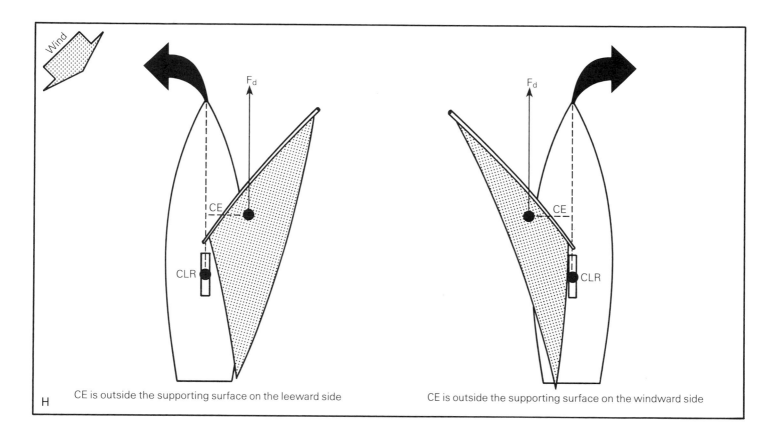

H | CE is outside the supporting surface on the leeward side | CE is outside the supporting surface on the windward side

described air currents also create lift L_s on the curved sail, which acts perpendicular to the direction of the apparent wind. A second parallelogram of forces can be constructed as in Fig. F from the drag or resistance R_s and the lift L_s to arrive at the total force F_t.

These forces of lift and drag relate to the curved sail alone, as if it were detached from the board. Unless another force is brought into the picture, the wind would drive the sailboard off in the direction of F_t. This sideways drifting, however, is opposed by the board's underwater profile, particularly the daggerboard and fin(s) since there is little 'hull' to speak of to add to the lateral resistance. The forces on the sail are transferred onto the board by the sailor's arms, legs and feet, as well as by the mast and mast pivot.

The total force F_t is considered to be the resultant of the forces acting on the board. Then, two components can be differentiated in the light of the above-mentioned resistance of the board to drift. There is first the driving component F_d which moves the board forward, and second there is the considerably greater transverse force F_h which is the cause

for the board's sideways drifting, and must be countered by the board, fin and daggerboard.

The previous discussions here have all dealt with closehauled sailing. On other courses less close to the wind, the transverse force decreases in favour of an increase in the driving force, until on a dead run both are acting in the same direction to drive the board forward (see page 46).

These forces, which have to be balanced on conventional sailboats for them to remain on a straight course without a great deal of rudder correction, actually represent the whole steering mechanism on the sailboard. Different imbalances can be brought about through raking the rig forward or backward, making the board steerable. The board will sail in a straight line only if a balanced situation is present between the total force of the sail and that of the hull (see page 70).

Fig. G illustrates different situations which one is likely to come across.

In (a), the total force of the sail, acting through the CE, is behind the CLR of the board, causing the board to head up into the wind.

In (b), the sail is in a balanced condition and both

forces lie on one line. The board moves ahead in a straight line.

In (c), the total force of the sail is located in front of the total hydrodynamic force and the board bears off, turning away from the wind.

Another important steering mechanism on a sailboard is the rotational moment of the sail, which is caused by the fact that the CE is not directly above the CLR. According to our view, not only the total force of the sail acts through the CE, but also its vector components. The driving force D_s acts on a point farther and farther off the centreline the more the sail is tilted to leeward.

Turning to windward results from this leeward, off-centre action of the forward driving force, out beyond the central position of the CLR, and the board heads up. This effect is particularly noticeable when beginners pull in the sail and start off.

The usual sailing position is different in higher wind speeds. The boardsailor pulls the sail way over to windward and enlarges the rotational torque of the body's centre of gravity. This makes the total force of the sail point higher than horizontal and this vertical component partly carries his weight. At the same time the driving force D_s again acts off-centre, but this time on the windward side, and causes the board to bear off to leeward.

This effect can be so strong in strong wind that the sail has to be pulled much further aft, in other words the CE has to be brought in such a position with respect to the CLR that the rotational effect is balanced out.

In order to sail as fast as possible one has to keep the forward propelling force D_s as great as possible, while minimizing all resistances and the transverse force F_h.

RACING

In 1984 in Los Angeles, a struggle for the Olympic precious metals is to take place. Windsurfing has achieved what no other sport in history has done: recognition as an Olympic discipline in fewer than fifteen years after its discovery. This shows the incredible development that the sport has received in its popularity, in the level of competition, and also in equipment production and internationality. In the meantime, along with class organizations there are many clubs which have tried to further the cause of this unique sport.

A few years ago, one seldom came across fellow boardsailors, whereas today many bodies of water are bustling with hundreds of enthusiastic participants. The Europeans are still the most numerous on the racing scene, but one is beginning to see participants from overseas and third-world countries more often.

Olympic Committee President Daume listed a few reasons for the acceptance of boardsailing into the Olympics. These were:

1. The high physical and psychological demands on the athletes.
2. Permanent installations, such as gymnasiums, tracks or fields are not necessary for training.
3. The relatively favourable purchase price and its corresponding wide distribution make it possible for sportsmen from poor countries to participate in the Olympic Games.
4. The simplicity of the equipment does not disadvantage the poorer countries as opposed to the highly technological nations.
5. Staging and conducting races for these 'boats' causes few financial or organizational problems for the host country.

Because there are no weight classes in the Olympics, it's going to be more difficult for the heavier sailors, who are often stronger physically, to win, in Los Angeles' light winds. The wind and sea conditions at future Olympic Games may favour those who are best suited, and accustomed, to heavy weather, however.

Note: Other signals may well be used, especially for course or safety instructions. Always check Race Instructions.

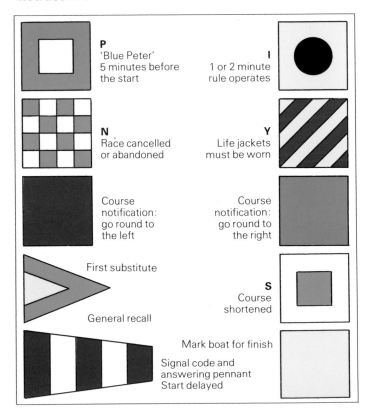

P
'Blue Peter'
5 minutes before
the start

I
1 or 2 minute
rule operates

N
Race cancelled
or abandoned

Y
Life jackets
must be worn

Course
notification:
go round to
the left

Course
notification:
go round to
the right

First substitute

S
Course
shortened

General recall

Mark boat for finish

Signal code and
answering pennant
Start delayed

Racing Courses

Triangular courses and variations thereof are now the most frequently seen, in boardsailing as for other racing, as they achieve the object of testing the competitors on beating to windward, reaching, and a downwind course that may present the alternatives of tacking downwind on a series of broad reaches or a dead run. Separate legs of the triangle, or the whole circuit, can be repeated as required. The turning marks and those for the start and finish lines, may be permanent or laid for each race. The start and finish lines may use marks on the triangle or be separate; they are aligned to allow the race officials to sight along them to spot boards that are across the line early at the start, and judge the order of finishing.

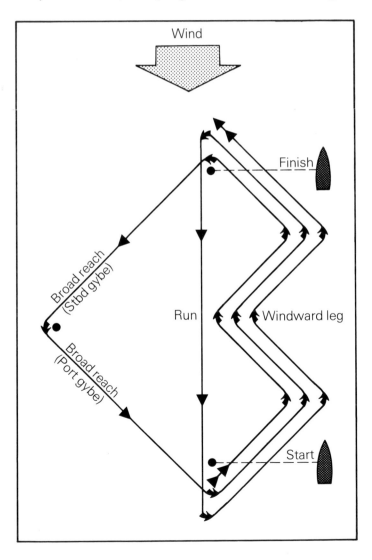

Race instructions

Although the actual racing will be conducted under the IYRU Racing Rules, competitors are also given instructions designed to inform them of many other general and particular facts and conditions. These will usually be printed, perhaps supplemented by others on a noticeboard, and the course instructions which may be displayed by a race committee boat or flagpole before the start. It is clearly essential to have obtained and studied all available instructions well before going afloat.

Race instructions fall into two categories. First, background information and instructions on the sailing area and organizing body's procedures and rules. This may include a sketch map and list of all the marks from which those for the race will be selected, local hazards and how one must sail with regard to them, mandatory personal buoyancy or safety equipment; signals to be used to denote classes, timing, which way round the course or marks; tide times. Second, details for a particular race or series: points scoring if used, any time limits, 720° turns or other penalties, etc. Reference is often made to the IYRU Rules, so these should be handy.

The course itself may be given well in advance or only shortly before the start, perhaps at the ten or five minute gun.

Points scoring

Where a series of races is held, points can be awarded according to the finishing order, with the winner receiving say zero and the others successively higher numbers. At the end of the series, the overall winner is the one who has accumulated the fewest points.

Various systems are used, depending on the event and country. The Olympics in 1984 will use the following scale:

1st place = 0
2nd place = 3
3rd place = 5.7
4th place = 8.5
6th place = 11.7

The seventh and subsequent finishers receive about 6 points more than their placing.

The Race Itself

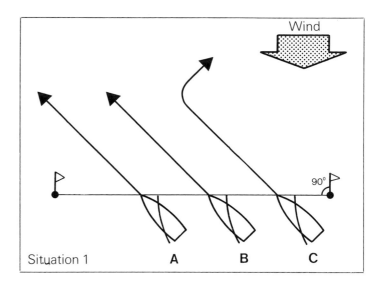

Situation 1

Choosing the starting position

Situation 1: The starting line is at right angles to the wind, and C is at an advantage over A and B. He can pursue his course if desired on starboard tack, or he can come about immediately if there is a wind shift.

Situation 2: Every race organizer tries to achieve the ideal case. The buoy on the left end of the line is placed somewhat ahead to avoid giving an advantage to any point on the line.

Situation 3: With a wind shift to the left, the sailors at the left end are better off. The position can become dangerous for A, since he must head up in order to get up to windward but can be covered by B, and thus risks hitting the mark. Very often, though, the entire group turns to the favoured side and the first leg is sailed on port tack.

The most important criteria at the start are the following: one's timing must result in being in the best starting position in relation to the tactical plan for the first leg, which will probably be sailed to windward. Exactly at the starting gun, the line has to be crossed there at full sailing speed. This is only possible if one can get, through knowing the racing rules and cold-blooded nerve, enough room to leeward (2–4 m) to bear off.

Following the starting signal, the most important thing is to concentrate on speed and acquiring some free space and clear wind. Then one can start worrying more about getting up to windward.

A lack of self-confidence, or doubting the wisdom of one's own decisions, lead to looking back too frequently and the loss of speed, which is a good way to get to the back of the fleet.

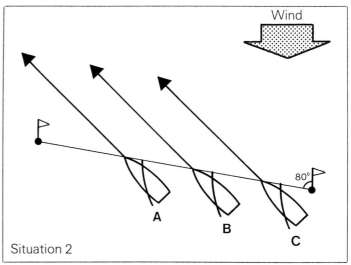

Situation 2

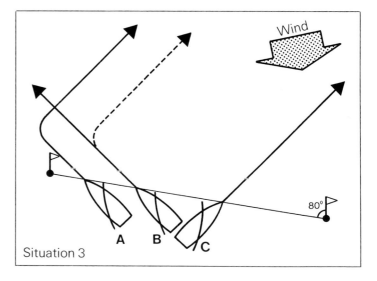

Situation 3

The upper photo series shows a perfect buoy rounding during one of the races in the 1980 Open Class World Championship in Israel. The sailor with sail number IS 10 has chosen the best approach arc to the buoy. By coming more from the outside, he can squeeze himself between the buoy and his opponents (F235) and put himself quite a few metres ahead of them.

The photomontage sequence below shows a fast course change as done on boards that resist turning quickly. This gybe is made with a mast hold. Tilting the sail so strongly forward towards the luff requires great care. The board must run level and the sail hand has to release the boom at the right time.

Timing before the start

The most decisive phase of a race is the start. One has to put together a tactical plan, choose a starting position, and then make sure of crossing the line after the expiration of the preparatory interval and exactly as the starting gun is fired.

Intense concentration, strong nerves and perfect board handling are the marks of a good racing sailor.

The boardsailor also has to calculate his drift, meaning how quickly he is displaced sideways or backwards by the wind and waves. Out on the sea, the tidal stream or current also makes it difficult sometimes to estimate the approach to the starting line. These races differ from other sailing races in that sailboards if well handled are considerably more manoeuvrable and thus a large part of the fleet of boards is already standing at the line before the start. The equipment is also not as likely to be damaged in possible collisions, and the damages are in any case smaller. The same right-of-way rules as for conventional sailboat racing are in effect, though, and the method of starting is also the same: ten minutes before the start there is a warning gun; five minutes before the start a second gun; then the starting signal itself.

During starts the one minute or five minute rule is very often used to keep the field more orderly and easier to control. These rules forbid crossing the starting line in *any* direction in the given period of time before the start. One cannot slide back over the line shortly before the start, squeeze out other sailors and thereby make an excellent start for oneself.

It is therefore a good idea to spend the last few minutes sailing very close to the wind below the starting line. By slightly heading up, it is possible to acquire some essential room to leeward in the last half minute before the start, in order to be able to bear off and pick up speed seconds before the starting signal. If one approaches the line or makes a start with too little speed, one usually falls back between the others and has to sail in their 'cut up' wind, with less chance of achieving a good result.

One can easily practice this creeping up to a particular point alone or with a few boardsailing friends. All that's needed is a reference point (marker or mooring buoys), an agreed period of time and a stopwatch, which is a necessity for every racing sailor. It takes a considerable amount of sensitivity and experience to get at the right angle to the wind and waves, and to be able to remain on course and also on time by slightly pulling in and letting out the sail to speed up or slow down. Nevertheless, in the process one must never lose one's manoeuvring ability by slowing down too much or stopping.

The upper series of pictures shows an unsuccessful start by the sailor in the foreground. The wind shifted to the right shortly before the starting signal and the participants on the leeward end of the starting line suddenly found themselves farther downwind of the next mark than the others. In such a situation one can hope that the wind will shift back, or else immediately decide to come about and sail off to the right.

The lower series shows Philip Pudenz (G 65) shortly before the start of the Windsurfing World Championship, Open Class, in Israel. The port side of the line was favoured and this caused a lot of crowding there. Those who positioned themselves too early near this end of the line could not hold a good position and drifted backward. G 65 has enough room and distance, and by the time the countdown is over he will have worked himself up to the port buoy, thereby achieving the best position.

Coming about with a mast hold

In a race, coming about is done like a move in chess — after thorough consideration. However, quite often one has to decide within seconds to tack, and only later does it become apparent whether the decision was right or wrong.

Excellent judgement and intuition are needed to place the windward legs and tacks. A decision to tack should only be made if there is enough space and if one doesn't have to give way to approaching boards.

Opponents who are ahead and to leeward can usually be readily observed and judging one's position in relation to them is simple. However, it be-

comes somewhat different with opponents to windward. It's not difficult to keep an eye on them in a light wind, but this becomes almost impossible in a strong wind because one has to concentrate on perfect sailing technique and the advantageous use of the waves. Therefore one has to keep the opponents' position in one's head, calculate the changes and effects of wind shifts and gusts, and be prepared to use defensive or offensive tactics.

Tacking in close quarters, such as keeping another board covered or fighting one's way up to someone by a quick double tack, requires concentrated observation of the opponent in order to be successful according to plan.

Beating

After an unsuccessful start, one has to escape the blanketing wind shadows and the other disturbed wind zones of the opponents. The diagram shows B in an area of cut up wind with a resulting disturbed air flow onto his sail. Depending on his tactical plan, he can tack to get clear, or get away by heading up somewhat at the cost of a slight loss in speed. Opponent C, on the other hand, can sail out of the wind shadow by bearing off and picking up speed for a short time with a little loss of distance made good to windward. But A may try to counter B's or C's attempts to escape, though at a likely cost to his own position. Struggles for position are especially common on the finishing beat, where everyone is trying to hold their position, or if they see a possibility, to attack and try to pass someone else.

The beating leg on inland water is sailed differently from one on the open sea. On inland water with gusts quickly following one another, the deciding factors between victory and defeat are often the talent for observation and the technique for coming about quickly. Every gust must be put to use at the right moment; for example, if a heading gust approaches from the front and forces one to bear off, one must tack at the start of the gust and thus gain some height to windward on the new tack. The smaller waves inland also make it possible to go windward well, since the sail can be kept in a constant optimal position to the wind.

On smaller lakes, where hills or buildings can create wind shadows or there are large wind shifts, the height gained can quickly be lost if one stops paying attention. On the contrary, there is usually a constant wind out on the sea and differences in speed result solely from the differing sailing techniques. The person who knows his sailboard best and steers with the greatest concentration will sail the fastest. Of course strategy and tactics also have a role, for example one's assessment of the consequences of the current or stream, and the placement of the beating legs with respect to the waves caused by the interaction of wind and tide, and perhaps an old swell. These may come from different directions and make difficult choppy water.

In such circumstances one usually looks for a compromise between gaining height to windward and greater speed. By sailing too high into the wind and as a result moving too slowly (pinching) the board can be shifted sideways strongly by the waves; or it meets the waves at too hard an angle and splashes down into the troughs, which has a stopping effect. Such mistakes can only be corrected by adjusting the sail's position and thus the air flow onto it, which leads ultimately to a loss in windward height and speed. A decisive lead can only be gained by sticking to the best compromise in heading and avoiding all unnecessary body and sail movements.

Rounding the first windward mark

On approaching the windward mark new considerations come into play, especially since one usually has a pretty good idea of one's position in a series (should this race be decisive, one has to concentrate more on direct opponents, known from their results in the intermediate races). If the fleet is approaching the buoy bunched up and from both sides, you should either be leading the group coming in on starboard tack or at least have a good position in it. A good eye and experience can really pay off in such a situation. If you cannot quite reach the buoy, you still have the right of way for the time being before the sailors on port tack, although the picture changes

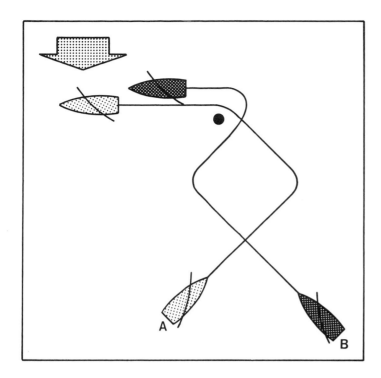

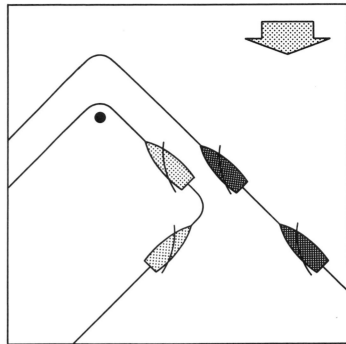

after coming about. One loses the better position by having to give way. Having to yield the right of way close to the buoy, with your sail fluttering and speed lost, and possibly having to allow other opponents to pass as well, is aggravating and can often tempt one into risky manoeuvres. So be sure before coming about that you will be able to make it past the buoy.

If a number of other boards with the right of way are approaching and all will be able to make it round the buoy, the one on port tack may be able to tack just underneath the leader of this group at the right moment. Skillful execution of the tack and observing the right-of-way rules are vital.

Sailors with the wind coming from starboard must not be forced to change direction by another board coming about on someone's bow. Tacking should be done slightly ahead and to leeward and the subsequent acceleration must occur smoothly and immediately, otherwise one risks being surrounded by those approaching.

If you have miscalculated and reach the buoy only with difficulty, you should never continue the tack to the bitter end. It's wiser to look for a place to come about early on and get in among those who will make the mark, than to try to pinch up to the buoy and possibly touch it. Re-rounding it as a penalty costs a lot of time and, even more important, places.

Broad reaching

Tactics on the broad-reaching legs depend on the conditions. In a steady wind it is better to sail direct to the mark, unless the waves or stream cause a change in the course actually sailed. If one's position is being threatened by an opponent, one has to try to get away from him through tactical measures. Such a situation, as well as the effects of any tidal stream and waves, makes deviations from the direct course necessary.

Sailing with the waves on broad reach is a lot of fun when racing and can give a big lead. However, it's not uncommon for competitors to be disqualified because of 'pumping'. In the future, the revised rules of the International Yacht Racing Union (IYRU) will be used; these state that pumping on a beat is forbidden. To initiate planing or surfing down a wave on a broad reach, one is permitted to pull in and let out the sail, at most, three times. Wind shifts should be exploited to achieve greater speed downwind. If gusts are approaching from astern, one heads up until they have arrived, then bears off and sails to leeward with them. The actual course then takes the form of a wavy line.

The decision to sail with or without the daggerboard down on a broad reach is important. A boardsailor using his daggerboard can point higher and

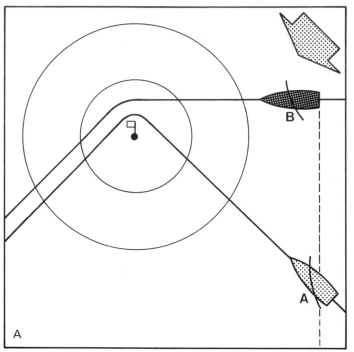

A

thus avert the attack of an opponent who has pulled up his daggerboard and is coming up from behind.

The small lateral surface of the attacker's board causes greater leeway when heading up and can lead to contact with an opponent. This is a violation of the racing rules and can lead to disqualification if the penalty 720° turn is not carried out.

If one is well behind and would like to pass a group of boards, a windward or leeward course remains as the alternative. The windward course is more favourable if the wind is blowing more from astern shortly after rounding the windward mark and shifts to come more from ahead at the end of the reaching leg. In the opposite wind conditions, it would be better to go downwind first and then gybe and approach the mark with greater speed. The basic requirements for this type of passing manoeuvre are the necessary lateral distance as one passes, avoiding the wind shadow, and an accurate estimation of the speed which one needs to make up for the detour.

The leeward course has the additional advantage of making it easier to get into the more favourable inner position at the mark, as demonstrated by the diagram. Board A has overlapped board B before reaching the outer circle, and therefore A has the right to sail on the inside at the mark and B must give him enough room to gybe round.

Sailing without a daggerboard

On sailboards without a pivoting centreboard, the daggerboard has to be pulled out in strong winds, on courses between a beam reach and running, to avoid capsizing. The inequality of pressure on the two sides of the daggerboard that is caused by the

sideways drift increases as a function of the speed. With a long lever arm (long daggerboard), a greater torque results and allows the board to capsize. Stronger loading on its windward or leeward side often has the same effect.

Sailing without a daggerboard requires much less concentration and a broad reach or running course can be mastered without great difficulty. It is only possible to sail without the daggerboard on the boards designed with flat bottoms, since the more rounded racing boards in the Open Class become very unstable and difficult to handle on such courses with the board removed. The elite sailors use pivoting centreboards that can be adjusted in area and position for different wind strengths.

Pulling out the daggerboard while sailing on a leg of a course is done as follows. After turning onto the reaching leg, continue for a little way with the board down. Then release the boom with the sail hand and with the mast hand pull the fluttering sail slightly to windward. The rig should be tilted against the wind so that the mast hand does not have to maintain a strong pull; only then can one stoop down and grab the strap or line that is attached to the top of the daggerboard. Lines covered by a plastic tube or reinforced with cloth tape, making a handle, are very popular. Those that lie too close to the board or are too short are difficult to catch hold of, and too thin ones cut into the back of the hand. Once pulled out of the slot, the freely-swinging daggerboard should never be held with the thumb, since it can be lost easily and cost a lot of places. It can be held better by putting the strap or line over the back of the hand and using the extended thumb to prevent it from slipping up to the elbow. There is a danger of injury when the daggerboard is hanging at the elbow, since at high speeds it is tossed about wildly when it touches the water.

Before the gybe, it is transferred from the sail hand to the mast hand, so that it will again be held by the sail hand once on the new tack.

The most difficult phase occurs at the end of the running leg. One must get ready to place the daggerboard back into its slot early enough, and then do it swiftly and with a sure grip, since everyone will be sailing closehauled immediately after the mark. With the daggerboard only half inserted, one loses distance to windward and risks contact with an opponent to leeward. Immediately after being placed back into the slot, it is pushed right down with the foot, so that manoeuvring can be done readily.

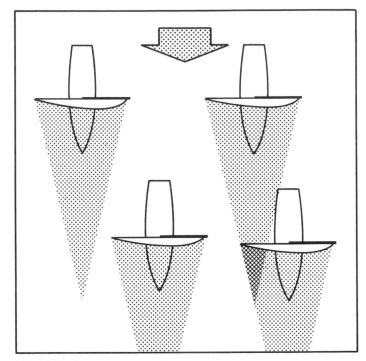

Windshadows on a running course

The running leg

The tactics on a run depend on the prevailing wind conditions. In a light wind, the direct course is most often sailed and one tries to get away from the wind shadows of the approaching sailboards by gybing as often as necessary. Increasing wind strengths (from Force 4 upwards) make tacking downwind possible

and despite the greater distance sailed, boards taking a direct course by running dead downwind to the mark can be passed. In high winds and waves one tries to surf with the waves while running.

Overall tactics

A race does not begin with the starting signal, but some time before. Getting warmed up and practising manoeuvres loosens and warms up the muscles which makes it easier to exert maximum effort without cramps during the race, and the balancing reactions are awakened. Furthermore, by sailing out early one has the chance to study the wind and waves and put together a tactical plan. If the marks have already been placed, it's not difficult to sight up to the windward mark, or to determine the favoured end of the starting line. When no favoured position can be recognized, it's best to stay close to one's toughest opponents. Should you end up in a bad starting position, it's much less frustrating if you are still in the vicinity of your direct opponents.

You should absolutely avoid being over the line, since the penalty is to sail a difficult course around the buoy or yacht marking the end of the line.

If the one or five minute rule is in effect, even after a correct start a competitor can be required to sail around a starting mark and cross the line once again. This penalises a violation of this rule during the countdown. Stricter one or five minute rules don't allow such compensation and a violation means disqualification. (The applicable rules will be found in the Race Instructions.) Adhering to the tactical plan and concentrating on speed should result in a good position at the first mark. Doubt always decreases one's performance and loses speed.

Near the first mark the position one has achieved can be estimated: further decisions are determined by this. If you are lying ahead of the fleet, the windward mark can also be approached on port tack without any problems. Should you be in the middle of the pack, it's advisable to round the buoy on starboard tack and thereby with the right of way over those on port.

In strong winds, the decision on whether the daggerboard should be pulled or pivoted up is made at the latest at the windward mark. This of course depends on one's class: Windsurfers and Windgliders are sailed with the daggerboard down, while in the Open Class practice varies. The daggerboard should be pulled up only if one is sure that the wind is strong enough to keep the board planing all the time.

The boardsailor ahead of you should be watched, and attacked at the right moment. Wind strengths over Force 5 require more physical stamina, and tactics play a lesser role. Falling in such high-speed sailing can cost one several hundred metres. Light and moderate winds, on the other hand, make it necessary to try to stay out of the wind shadows of the others in order to be able to risk passing to leeward or windward, or to attain the inner position in rounding the gybing mark.

On a running course, one also has the chance to blanket the leader and take away some of his speed, and then possibly pass him in a surprise manoeuvre. If one is far behind, an attempt can be risked to pass a group of opponents by tacking downwind, weighing the increased distance to be sailed against the advantage of greater speed.

Final windward leg

The struggle for the coveted inner position begins anew at the end of the downwind leg. The properly timed demand for enough room can put one in a good position to round the mark cleanly. Coming from the outside, one can still attain the inner position through skillful gybing, shortly before the mark. The ensuing beat to the finish line, particularly in the last decisive race of a series, often consists of pairs of competitors racing against each other. These close tactics require constant observation of one's opponent in order to keep him under control and not to be fooled by any faked manoeuvres. Unnecessarily close battling leads not only to hard feelings, but often to a poorer placing also. Aside from these considerations, the position of the finishing line should be judged immediately after rounding the last mark, and the quickest way to it should be worked out.

As each board crosses the line it is confirmed as finishing by the boat positioned there, which usually sounds a horn. Any protest against another sailor must be made immediately after crossing the finish line. Declarations must normally be signed on coming ashore, and any other provisions followed according to the Race Instructions for the event.

Do it standing up. Karl Messmer at Diamond Head (next page)

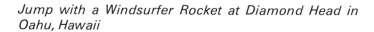
Jump with a Windsurfer Rocket at Diamond Head in Oahu, Hawaii

(Next pages)

In racing in strong wind, there is a manoeuvre that can be used to catch one's breath. When one's position is not under pressure, the best thing is to sail through a bigger arc when gybing. By this means one can relieve the tensed body stance of the broad reach, relax the muscles and prepare mentally for rounding the upcoming mark cleanly.

Through haste and a rushed move, or worse, a fall, one can lose more than by beginning the gybe earlier. In addition, the breather lets one continue sailing on the new course with renewed strength.

Particularly in high waves, it becomes important to carry out the gybe in good time and in the proper

place. By surfing on a wave, the increased speed and diminished pressure on the sail facilitate the manoeuvre.

The greatest caution should be taken at the leeward mark so as not to shoot past it with too much speed and lose valuable distance to windward.

1

2

360° Turn

This manoeuvre can be seen not only in freestyle events but especially during races. It is used as a penalty for rule violations, where a double turn (720°) is required. It must be executed swiftly to limit the time lost, as well as the loss of valuable distance. It's also a good training manoeuvre, since it requires complete command of the sailboard.

1. The manoeuvre is begun by heading up, as in a fast tack.
2, 3. The bow turns through the wind as the sail is pulled way across the board. The sailor then moves in front of the mast.
4. While standing on the board's front half, push it round underneath the sail with the feet. The board turns easily since there are no lateral surfaces on its front half to resist the sideways pres-

5

6

3

4

sure of the feet. *Be careful*, because the board can start moving backwards during this phase!

6. During the turn, one has to adjust one's position to the board's rotation. The body position in relation to the rig does not change.

7. The initial position can be reached quickly from this running position by forcefully heading up into the wind and pressing on the board's lee edge.

Carrying this out in a strong wind requires considerably more agility. One assumes a deep squat to reduce the chances of falling. If the balance is still shaky, sit down near the daggerboard slot for a moment. If the force of the lateral pull is still too great, the sail hand should let go of the boom. The mast hand continues to keep the mast upright, so one can start again immediately once the difficulties have been overcome.

7

8

Slalom Racing

The Windsurfer World Championships include in the programme a slalom race around buoys, along with the long-distance race and freestyle competition. Slalom racing is excellent for mastering coming about

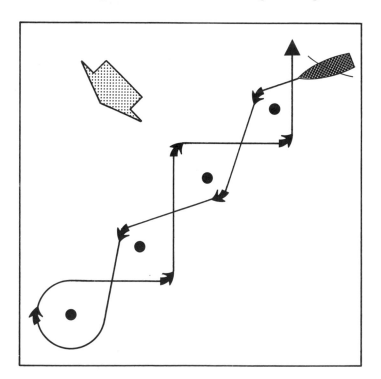

and gybing in the smallest of spaces. The direct competition between opponents afforded by side-by-side courses emphasizes speed, precision and great dexterity. The manoeuvres must be thought out and cleanly executed under the pressure of time, since one can be left far behind after a fall or a drop in speed, and not qualify for the next round in the knockout elimination system.

The 1980 World Championships in the Bahamas lasted for one and a half days because of the large entry of 300 registered participants. At the end, Robby Naish and Mike Waltze remained pitted against each other and fought an exciting slalom duel, which Naish was able to win.

For beginning racing sailors, this type of training is best suited for mastering the various manoeuvres. Four or five buoys on a course are necessary as well as the same number of weights to weigh their ground line down, which ought to be about 80 m long. An anchor with a line as long as the water's depth will hold the line of floats in the wind. A second course laid parallel to the first allows the additional possibility of sailing diagonally up and down. Boardsailing clubs could well incorporate this as a training method in their beginners' programmes, in view of the practice of including this type of racing in some top-class events. Such side-by-side racing is also a lot of fun for both youngsters and adults, and they learn the manoeuvring technique without even trying.

TRICK SAILING

Head dip

This freestyle stunt is relatively easy and can be used as practice for a water start. Frequently one falls into the water because of having pulled back to windward too vigorously, destroying the air flow onto the sail. When a head dip is performed correctly, the sail is let out for a moment and as the pressure on it decreases the sailor dips his head into the water.

Then he trims the sail in again and pulls himself back up with the boom.

Everyone who has mastered the essential basic techniques will someday want to increase his repertoire with a few stunts. 'Trick surfing' is also called 'freestyle', which expresses the fact that it has no set limits. With time, however, a few manoeuvres have become classics and are performed at special championships and judged according to a points system. As in trick skiing or 'hot dogging', yet more spectacular stunts are always being presented and their number is steadily growing.

The tricks described here are primarily exercises to develop the necessary skill in handling the board and a good sailor should be able to perform them. Through working to perfect them, he can learn to manoeuvre his board exactly and effortlessly and they can sometimes give a valuable advantage in difficulty situations in a race.

A start directly out of the water is the most elegant way of starting after a windward fall. Allowing oneself to be pulled up onto the board by the wind's force and to sail off at full speed is extremely impressive.

As difficult as it may seem, this trick can easily be learned on the beach, with enough wind. With the rig placed in the beam-reaching position, one leans far back until the diminishing sail pressure allows one to fall back, and finally sits in the sand. To stand up, it is enough to lift the arms up somewhat and bend the legs at the same time, thereby shortening the load and allowing the wind coming into the sail to pull one up into the normal sailing position.

One can create a situation which simulates these conditions by putting the whole board on the beach in the beam-reaching position. This has the advantage of allowing one to determine the right position for the feet. Go through the sequence slowly in the

Water start

In this photomontage sequence, note the position of the feet as they try to keep the board across the wind. The arms control the sail and try to find the proper

angle. The sailor waits for a gust, then brings his centre of gravity closer to the board and forces himself to be pulled up by pulling in with the sail hand. The increasing sail pressure pulls him effortlessly onto the board.

mind first: to sit down, the sail is let out slightly and simultaneously the body leans far back. While lying on the sand, try to find the right position for the sail by letting it out and pulling it in. The arms then push the sail up and the body's centre of gravity is brought closer to the board by bending the legs. The wind automatically provides the necessary assistance for standing up.

The next step is starting in the water. The only new problem that arises is holding the board in the beam-reaching position with the feet. If the previous exercise is exploited, it should be relatively easy to keep the board at the proper angle. In winds of Force 4—5 the start works without any problems. Sufficient lateral surface and a normal sized dagger-board and fins are a prerequisite, otherwise the board slides vigorously off to the side. The ideal water depth for practising is waist to chest high. The rig can be easily held over the head and there is no

difficulty in placing first one foot and then the other on the board's edge. There are usually more problems in deep water, since in order to sit down to windward, one usually falls back too vigorously and pulls the sail down flat onto the water's surface. Then attempting to push it up is useless.

Mastering the water start can score points, whether at a freestyle show, in a race following a windward fall or from amazed friends. With the less buoyant boards it is the best way to get moving, as they will tend to submerge if standing still under a person's weight.

'Towing' on Lake Garda

Sailing backwards outside the boom (upper left)

Stand to windward, back to the sail. The starting position is from the basic stance, however with one's back to the sail. The front hand reaches backward and grasps the boom about 1 foot (30 cm) from the mast. Just as when starting in the normal position, the mast hand pulls the rig past the body, the upper torso bends forward slightly, and simultaneously the sail hand grasps the boom with an underhand grip. It seems at first that you will dive into the water, but the sail hand can still regulate the sail's pressure, and one hangs in equilibrium turned around on the windward side.

Sailing backwards inside the boom (lower left)

Again, the initial phase begins with the basic start position. The front hand holds the rig by the uphaul, while the back hand holds the wishbone with an underhand grip. Releasing the uphaul and turning 180° allows one to duck under in between the sail and the boom. Then lean forward and push the boom to windward. The feet should be securely placed in the middle of the board. The sail hand compensates for gusts, although it is somewhat limited by the lack of space. So, to let out the sail farther the upper torso has to be turned to the back.

Pictured here is the Italian, Fabio Bellini (1980 European Champion in the Windsurfer Class), in perfect form during the 1980 Windsurfer World Championships in the Bahamas.

Variations on rail riding

Sailing on the lee side

This trick can be done standing on the inside as well as the outside of the boom. The body leans with the back against the sail or the boom, but only as strongly as the wind is pushing it over from the windward side.

One's view is limited, though, and one should learn and practise this stunt only at a safe distance from obstacles and any other sailing craft.

Standing with the back against the sail, either on the inside or the outside of the wishbone, presents new problems for the sailor. To equalize the sail's pulling force, the arms pull or push the boom to windward, so that it is balanced by the body. This position and the unusual movements are a quite new experience. One should only attempt this exercise after acquiring perfect mastery of sailing in the normal position in winds of any strength.

WINDSURFING PHOTOGRAPHY

If you walk along the beach on a beautiful board-sailing day, you'll be surprised to discover that the camera is just as important to most sailors as a trapeze or daggerboard. One can speculate that this fact has its roots in the social, psychological or 'pseudological' aspects of this special group in society. Indeed, most of them have just as much fun taking pictures as 'taming the wind with their bare hands'. To let as little as possible interfere with this pleasure, we will consider some of the special problems of boardsailing photography in the following section.

Cameras, whether for movies or still photos, are sensitive instruments made of high quality materials and constructed with the utmost precision. The precisely made and close-fitting components of the diaphragm and shutter can become unusable in a short time because of corrosion. The cause of corrosion, in most cases, is excessive moisture, considerably augmented by salt and electrical potentials.

These triggering elements are found exactly where sailing photographers gather. On the sea, the camera is confronted with flying spray, water and salty air; on the beach, with sand in addition. Fresh water conditions are only slightly less destructive. Most ambitious photographers have good equipment which contains one or more batteries, quite enough to speed up the destruction process greatly. A camera that falls in the water, if only for a few moments, becomes unusable within seconds, and may be permanently ruined. It helps very little to take it apart and blow it dry. In order to be armed against such danger, and not to allow the fun of sailing and surfing photography to be spoiled, we will discuss different aspects of camera protection.

Protecting the camera

It doesn't help to insure one's equipment well, and then with the thought of having nothing to lose, handle it carelessly. Such an accident on the second or third day of a Caribbean vacation will quickly make the rest of the time become 'a unique and unforgettable experience'. A protective cover against the water is therefore necessary.

Four possibilities, which have different records of success, are: the 'true' underwater housing, the home-made kind, the underwater bag from Ewa-Marine Co., and the all-weather camera.

Let's start with the simplest and the cheapest solution — the Ewa-Marine bag, a simple but effective protection against water and sand. The bag is made of see-through vinyl and has plenty of room for a camera. The upper edge has a double bar, which when screwed together closes the bag's opening tightly. It's such a tight closure that the manufacturer even recommends it for use as a diving housing for up to 10 metres depth of water. A glove is incorporated in the bag's side, allowing one to shoot and manipulate the camera in the bag. In order not to affect the optical quality too much, a piece of glass is sealed into the front side, and large enough to give a clear view for most of the commonly used lenses. For a better look into the viewfinder there is also a glass disc in the back of the bag. All in all, this underwater housing is well made and offers sufficient protection from water and sand at a reasonable price.

However, in practice, holding onto and shooting the camera is not quite as easy as it sounds. Because the camera is not fixed in the bag but held only by the hand in the glove, and supported by the other hand on the outside, the two pieces of glass in front of the lens and viewfinder very easily become displaced or angled. Aside from this, there is the danger of light reflections getting into the picture, because there is no way to attach a sun shade. Adjusting the shutter speed and the diaphragm with the gloved 'inner' hand is not exactly easy and the use of a fixed-focus setting is recommended (and explained below).

Though this is a very reasonably priced method of protecting most cameras, nevertheless working with it does take some getting used to.

The next mode of protection is the most expensive, and at the same time the safest: namely the

One has to be as close as possible to the action to shoot such spectacular pictures. A measure of courage and, above all, good physical condition are needed to wait for hours in breaking waves and raging water masses for a good shot.

(next page)
A jump by Robby Naish in the waves of Kailua, divided into separate phases to show the enormous acrobatic and athletic feat of this exercise (next page)

acquisition of a really waterproof underwater housing as is used in diving. These are usually made of aluminium and are designed for the individual camera and its flash unit. Anyone who is interested in such equipment should enquire about the underwater housing made by Oceanic Co.

In the interest of the majority of surfing and boardsailing photographers, however, we will direct our attention to more affordable products. The Ikelite Co. sells camera housings made of shockproof transparent plastic, which are extremely well made and function exceptionally well. The housing consists of two bowl-shaped halves that are tightly fastened with stainless steel V2A latches. To make the case truly waterproof, O-rings are used at the joints. These insure that no drop of water gets in even at a depth of 100 metres.

A replaceable dome is located on the case's front side, into which the lens projects. Various domes are available so that lenses of various focal lengths can be used without undesireable shadows appearing. Usually a simple dome is used for normal and shorter telephoto lenses. However, a wide-angle dome should also be purchased; it has an arched front disc and can be used with lenses down to 17 mm focal length. Especially dynamic views are best taken from in the water.

The Ikelite housing is available for practically all types of cameras. Big price differences result from the different features necessary for particular camera types. Units for professional motorized equipment are naturally expensive, whereas simple cameras can be 'dressed' at far less cost.

For those who take pictures only for memories, and haven't got it into their heads to reap money and fame with them, there is another very adequate solution. Take a simple pocket camera and purchase an underwater casing for it, from almost any photographic shops. The strong transparent shell holds and transfers adjustments to the small camera and is easy to pack and take along. The fact that one has to be satisfied with photos that cannot be enlarged into posters is acceptable in view of its convenience and ease of use.

There are also many people in sailing circles who believe that with a little effort, but for a lot less money, practically anything can be made at home. The following section, written for this group, has instructions for constructing a basic underwater housing which has already been tested and proven, for motor-driven cameras.

The materials needed are: clear Perspex, plexiglass or polycarbonate sheet about 8–10 mm thick; a short tube of the same sort of material and corresponding in length and diameter to the lens used; and in addition six V2A latches, foam rubber, soft rubber for seals, and a cement that will join the plastic parts. The V2A latches can be purchased in any good diving store.

The housing itself is a simple square box with a large lid. On the opposite side, the section of plastic tube is attached, to serve as a lens dome.

First of all, the camera along with its motor are measured to insure a proper fit. This will determine the height and width of the box. At the place where the lens will be located, a perfectly round hole is cut in the side, of the same diameter as the tube's outside diameter. The tube is then inserted and fixed with cement, following its instructions for use exactly. A round piece of the plastic sheet is then glued to the tube's front side. The sawn-out piece should not be used: instead, use a piece 4 mm thick, to give better optical qualities. This work should be carried out very carefully because excess glue or dirt will eventually be difficult to remove without leaving scratches on the front disc.

The V2A latches are then screwed onto the lid and the box, that is, the latches onto the lid and the clamp on the box's side. Before putting the parts together glue a small strip of waterproofing soft rubber (not foam rubber) between the lid and the box. This sealing strip should be coated with a bit of silicone grease to make an absolutely waterproof closure. (However, take extreme care to keep silicone grease off the lens area of the box, or the camera itself: it is impossible to remove.)

After having finished the box, lid and 'dome', begin to pad the box's inside with foam rubber. The foam rubber should be arranged so that the camera can be pressed into the housing and be securely seated. The lens of the camera should be aligned with the centre of the dome as far as possible.

The shutter release button is then added. A release button for a pocket camera can be purchased in a diving store: it is a simple wire shaft with a rubber button. This button is fastened through the housing wall as near as possible to the camera's trigger.

That does it. Of course, one can add a handle and a carrying belt. As mentioned before, this is only a rough description and anyone who follows it must take his camera's individual features into consideration.

One more comment about housings. While photographing sailing or surfing, the lens area usually becomes wet from spray, which compromises its optical quality considerably. What can be done about this? NASA developed a compound with which the windows of the space capsules were coated, in order to keep them free of rain and spray when the astronauts plunged into the sea and were looking for their rescuers. This fluid can be purchased in some car shops, for a lot of money, and it really works. It is sold under the name of 'Rain Free' in 150 ml blue bottles.

An old solution is available, however, for those, who don't care to pay so much. One simply spits on the disc, rubs it around and rinses it with some water. This is a trick from diving, where divers do this to the insides of their facemasks and goggles in order to see clearly under water. However, the effect isn't very long lasting.

Next to the three possibilities mentioned, of placing the camera in a housing and thereby having a fairly difficult time working with it, there is available yet another very acceptable method for sailing or diving photography, the Nikonos. As can be guessed from the name, the Nikon Co. has a camera that was especially designed for diving and all-weather use. Conceptually, it's a very simple camera, without light or distance meters and with a simple viewfinder. Its simplicity allows great reliability and robustness, allowing one to do practically anything with it. This piece of equipment is insensitive to water and sand, snow or cold, and is the ideal companion for all those who participate in sports, particularly boardsailors and sailors on bigger craft.

The exposure time required for the situation has to be set and then because of the resulting fix-focus setting the Nikonos is always ready for use. Unfortunately, there are only two lenses available for this camera, one of which, the 80 mm, is eliminated for most people because of the difficulty of working it. The 35 mm wide-angle lens, on the other hand, is truly super.

The Nikonos is not exactly inexpensive, at first glance, although the investment pays for itself in a short time if one takes a lot of photos.

The Fujica Co. sells a somewhat cheaper all-weather camera which is waterproof and has automatic exposure, although its photographic quality is not very high. Somewhat less expensive is a pocket camera from Minolta. Because of the smaller size of its film, the usual drawbacks such as reduced sharpness and grain appear in the pictures, once enlarged.

How does one take photographs with such a camera, then, one on which the adjustment capabilities have been either limited or altered? Using a fix-focus setting has turned out to be the most satisfactory method. The focus and the aperture opening are set so that one has a great possible range due to a large depth of field, thus making constant adjustment of the focus unnecessary. For example, at an exposure time of 1/125 sec, one can adjust the depth of field to be sharp from 2 metres to infinity, using a 28 mm wide-angle lens. Wide-angle lenses are better suited for this method due to their longer focal lengths.

The proper exposure time also has to be chosen for boardsailing or surfing photos. Obviously, one is dealing with a very fast sport, and can easily get blurring with too long exposure times. Therefore, one should never expose for longer than 1/125 sec, and possibly even shorten the exposure time further by the choice of faster film. 19 DIN 64 ASA film is well suited for transparencies as well as negatives, and in clear sunshine always permits an acceptable exposure time. Should there be less light available due to clouds or the time of day, 27 DIN 400 ASA film will give good results. One should also note that it is cheaper to shoot film for transparencies (positives) than negatives; slides can also be projected and enlarged, and have at least the same quality as is usually got from negatives. If desired, prints can be made from transparencies as well as from negatives.

What does one photograph? Ideally, whatever catches your interest. Just press the release button often and don't try to set things up too much. It's a lot better to have something worth seeing on the photo than just a lot of posing. Friends, girlfriends or other sailors and their boards are often more interesting than, for instance, a carefully planned back-lighted shot of a static boardsailor.

THE OLYMPIC BOARD

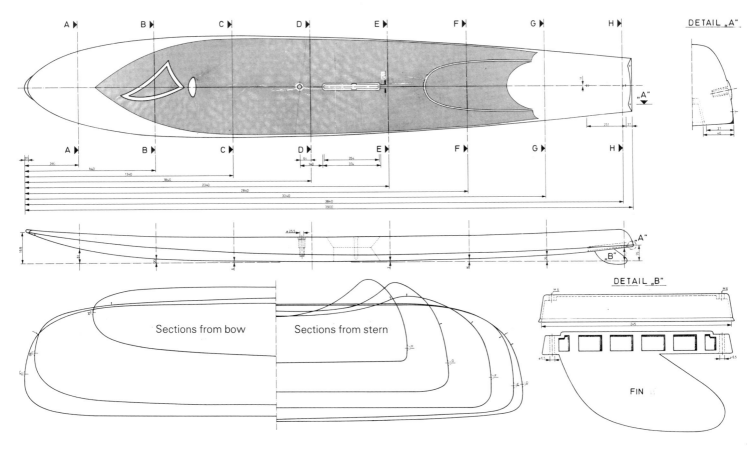

DETAIL „A"

DETAIL „B"

Sections from bow   Sections from stern

FIN

The IYRU decided at its annual meeting in 1980 in London to give Olympic status to the international Windglider class for the Summer Olympics in 1984, in Los Angeles.

Technical data and plan of the Windglider

Length: 3.90 m
Width: 0.65 m
Depth: 0.15 m
Volume: 230 L
Weight: 21–24 kg
Sail area: approximately 6.8 m²
Material: GRP (fibreglass)

CHAMPIONSHIPS

OPEN CLASS, WINDSURFER, WINDGLIDER AND SEA PANTHER CHAMPIONSHIP RESULTS

Open Class	Heavyweight Class	Lightweight Class	Ladies
United Kingdom			
1980 Torbay	J. Stacey M. Todd *Equal First*	J. Turner	F. Mackay
1980 Heineken Series	P. Caldwell C. Clements M. Todd	G. Fuller G. Turner K. Blake	D. Shoreland L. Openshaw L. Vincent
1981 Blackpool	L. Noble P. Caldwell G. Aldous	G. Fuller J. Swain R. Tushingham	F. Mackay L. Ryder C. Seeger Equal L. Richardson Third
1982 Porthpean, Cornwall	L. Noble C. Watson D. Perks	A. Biggs G. Fuller S. Sawyer	J. Martin C. Seeger A. Noble
European Championships			
1980	K. Messmer CH M. Gerard F R. Nagy F	J. Wangaard NL P. Pudenz D J. v.d. Starre NL	A. Maus F A. v. d. Starre NL A. Vos NL
1981	K. Messmer CH F. Spöttel D S. v.d. Berg NL	T. Staltmaier D H. Borde F P. Villier F	M. Graveline F E. Stehle D P. Toschi I
World Championships			
1979 Guadeloupe	K. Messmer CH P. Galas F N. Stickl D		A. Maus F R. Smith USA M. Graveline F
1980 Israel	K. Messmer CH S. v.d. Berg NL R. Nagy F	T. Staltmaier D J. Myrin S H. Borde F	M. Graveline F N. Johnson USA A. Maus F
1981 Florida	J. Wangaard NL F. Gautier F P. Villier F	S. v.d. Berg NL R. Naish USA K. Messmer CH	M. Berner N N. Johnson USA M. Graveline F

Windsurfer

	Weight Class A	B	C	D	Ladies

U.K. Championship

	A	B	C	D	Ladies
1979 Paignton	G. Fuller N. Tillet J. Howgarth	P. Vivian C. Clements A. Alfred	M. Middleton P. Coul K. Enevoldsen	M. Todd A. Dovey M. Von Bertele	F. Mackay R. Eslava L. Vincent
1980 Mounts Bay	G. Fuller* J. Turner B. Oakley	S. Avery *Overall Champion	R. Smith P. Caldwell	C. Clements M. Todd A. Dovey	L. Vincent J. Ellis
1981 Weymouth	N. Tillett G. Fuller D. Smith	B. Oakley G. Wilcocks P. Vivian	D. Caldwell P. Caldwell J. Kirschner	C. Clements K. Enevoldsen Brooks	P. Way F. Mackay L. Vincent
1982 Sandgate, Kent	N. Tillet G. Fuller D. Adams	G. Wilcox P. Thorn C. Laurens	G. Aldous S. Avery R. Smith	J. Facey J. Simmons T. Ball	P. Way L. Rackham C. Paxman

European Championship

	A	B	C	D	Ladies
1978	K. Messmer CH M. Nieuwbourg F R. Nagy F	D. Le Bihan F L. Langlois F J.-M. Fabre F	H. Borde F M. Garaudee F D. Magnan F	A. Foyen N H. d. Maar NL A. Herberger D	M. Graveline F B. Thijs NL C. Feuillerat F
1979	K. Messmer CH S. Descorps F O. Tellier NL	D. Le Bihan F R. Nagy F T. Staltmaier D	J. Myrin S N. Stickl D J. v.d. Starre NL	D. Baer CH A. Foyen N K. v.Spronson NL	M. Graveline F M. Maus F B. Thijs NL
1980	K. Messmer CH M. Nieuwbourg F N. Olivari I	F. Gautier F J.P. Boghossian F R. Nagy F	T. Staltmaier D D. Le Bihan F J. Myrin S	P. Brianda I A. Herberger D P. O. Skaaret N	M. Graveline F M. Maus F L. Gorgerino I
1981	G. Calvet F K. Messmer CH I. Bourne F	G. Masters AUS J.P. Boghossian F P. Mani F	J. Wangaard NL J. Myrin S F. Gautier F	T. Staltmaier D D. Caldwell G.B. N. Sayre USA	M. Graveline F P. Way G.B. L. Gorgerino I

World Championship

	A	B	C	D	Ladies
1978 Mexico	R. Naish USA G. Hyde AUS O. Tellier NL	M. Schweitzer USA N. Stickl D P. Love USA	A. Foyen N P. Pudenz D H. Peeters B	T. Myrin S K. Winner USA M. Garaudee F	B. Thijs NL M. Graveline F R. Smith USA
1979 Greece	M. Nieuwbourg F S. Descorps F R. Naish USA	T. Eude F N. Stickl D M. Bouwmeester NL	J. Salen S J. Myrin S T. Staltmaier G	C. Larned USA M. Schimkus D M. Weyers NL	M. Graveline F A. v.d. Starre NL R. Smith USA
1980 Bahamas	K. Messmer CH G. Calvet F G. Aguera USA	F. Gautier F J.-P. Boghossian F A. Nilson S	T. Staltmaier D J. Myrin S M. Garaudee F	G. Long USA P. Villier F A. Foyen N	M. Mascia I N. Johnson USA M. Berner NL
1981 Okinawa	M. Waltze USA J. Mouret F G. Calvet F	R. Nagy F G. Butchart AUS G. Aguera USA	F. Gautier F R. Wilmot AUS M. Schweitzer USA	J. Myrin S N. Sayre USA T. Persson S	M. Mascia I R. Smith USA L. Gorgerino I

Windglider

U.K. Championship

U.K. Championship	Heavyweight	Lightweight	Ladies	Youth
1980	D. Smart A. Shoreland D. Northway	R. James M. Shoreland G. Davies	D. Shoreland A. Ballard G. Wilkinson-Cox	D. Harvey S. Priestly C. Dow
1981 Hayling Island	J. Facey P. Tyles D. Smart	B. Oakley N. Tillet M. Shoreland	C. Seeger D. Shoreland	*Overall Winners* J. Facey B. Oakley N. Tillet
1982 Torquay	M. Shoreland A. Shoreland D. Smart	N. Tillet S. Priestly R. Harris	D. Shoreland S. Mitchell J. Stock	S. Priestly P. Sciblia G. Burnside

European Championships

European Championships	Lightweight	Heavyweight	Ladies
1978 Port Grimaud	H. Borde F D. Burkert D P. Galas F	D. Thijs NL L. Gertler D M. Hinz D	D. Martin D H. Karrer D B. Thijs NL
1979 Travemünde	S. v.d. Berg NL N. Stickl D C. Haglund S	F. Peusch D. Thijs NL K. Maran I	M. Graveline F B. Thijs NL A. Maus F
1980 Holland	S. v.d. Berg NL H.P. Michel CH R. v.d. Berg	D. Thijs NL F. Peusch D T. Aagesen DK	A. Jansen NL B. Thijs NL S. v.d. Aalst NL
1981 Gardasee	S. v.d. Berg NL M. Tellier NL F. Spöttel D	P. Villier F O. Tellier NL K. Maran I	A. Maus F M. Berner N C. v.d. Paer B

World Championships

World Championships	Weight Classes A	B	C	D	Ladies
1978 Martinique	Y. Roussel F H. Borde F C. Haglund S	P. Hayot F W. Raudaschl A J.-F. Hayot F	K.-H. Stickl D J.-C. Desgrottes F J.-P. Deldatto F	D. Thijs NL R. le Dauphin F T. Ernst D	A. Maus F B. Thijs NL T. Cousin F
1979 Mauritius	S. v.d. Berg NL J.-M. Rouillard Maur. R. Bamrung Thai	Kl. Maran I F. Peusch D J.-P. Rouillard Maur			A. Jansen NL C. Leisegang D H. Karrer D
1980 Plattensee	S. v.d. Berg NL R. Brock D F. d. Groot NL	K. Maran I D. Thijs NL T. Aagesen DK			U. Huber A B. Thijs NL A. Jansen NL
1981 Palamos	S. v.d. Berg NL A. Mamusa I H. Borde F	V. Borde F P. Villier F T. Staltmaier D			A. Kölbach D R. Lammerichs- Heuer D N. Johnson USA

Sea Panther

U.K.	Men		Ladies		Youth (M & F)
1979–80 Frostbite Series	A. White J. Payne A. Hyndes		K. Hyndes E. Iversen N. Gotham		
1980 Championships	A. White J. Hoggarth D. Smith		E. Robinson M. Atha L. Evans		J. Hoggarth G. McKinlay D. Trainer
1980–81 Frostbite Series	G. Way A. White G. McKinlay		L. Packham L. Evans M. Atha		

	Heavyweight	Lightweight	Ladies	Senior	Youth
1981 Rutland Water	S. Keightly P. Caldwell D. Perks	J. Chesborough D. Smith J. Swain	L. Rackham P. Way F. Mackay	K. Reed J. Richardson S. Linley	D. Traynor J. Langford R. Longstaff
1982 Grafham Water	M. Neale C. Helps D. Caldwell	M. Playle D. Smith M. Longstaff	F. Longstaff L. Robinson S. Sinclair	J. Blain	D. Hale J. Longford R. Longstaff

A — Austria	CH — Switzerland	I — Italy	NL — Netherlands	THAI — Thailand
AUS — Australia	D — Germany	J — Japan	PUR — Puerto Rico	UK — United Kingdom
B — Belgium	DK — Denmark	Maur — Mauritius	S — Sweden	USA — United States
CAN — Canada	F — France	N — Norway	SP — Spain	

ACKNOWLEDGEMENTS

The authors and the publisher would like to thank all those without whose generous help this publication could not have been possible: Tilo Schneckenburger, Hole Rössler, Karl Messmer and Michael Nissen for text contributions; Eckart Wagner for his technical advice; and the Nikon Co. AG in Küssnacht for their friendly support.

Special thanks are due to Photo Reger Co. in München for their generous help with the lab work.

Photomontages: Yves Buchheim
Illustrations: Ronald Sautebin
Layout and design: Yves Buchheim
English translation: Judit Farkas

Colour lithographs: Vaccari Zinco-Grafica, Modena
Black and white lithographs: Atesa Argraf SA, Geneva
Typesetting: Tameside Filmsetting Ltd, Ashton-under-Lyne
Printing and Binding: G. J. Manz Aktiengesellschaft, München-Dillingen/Do.

After you've read Windsurfing Technique, you'll be ready for more . . .

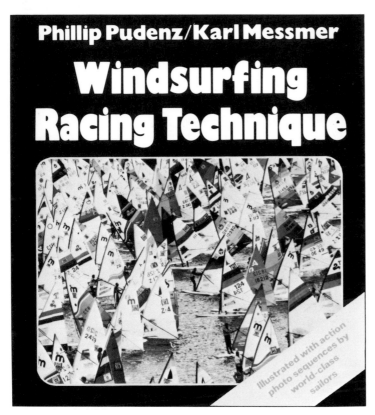

Phillip Pudenz / Karl Messmer

Windsurfing Racing Technique

Illustrated with action photo sequences by world-class sailors

WINDSURFING RACING TECHNIQUE
Philip Pudenz and Karl Messmer

Two of the world's top sailors analyse, explain and demonstrate the techniques needed for race winning – fast tacking and gybing, speed, mark rounding, 720° turns, trapezing, sail/board trim, starts, tactics and picking the best courses.

Racing courses, signals, scoring, protests and the racing rules particular to windsurfing are all covered, so getting started in racing, or improving your results, are made easier.

Tandem boards also have their own special sailing techniques, for both speed and manoeuvring. Here, you can learn them from the experts.

Dozens of colour and black/white photos are sequences by Michael Garff make this a unique book.

Hardback, 180 pages

SAILBOARDS CUSTOM-MADE
Hans Fichtner and Michael Garff

Do-it-yourself sailboard building is a practical, economical way of having a jumping or fun board, one for the kids to learn on, or to try out your own ideas. Hans Fichtner is a shaper for Mistral, and here he explains step by step the methods and tools that are most suitable for amateur builders and will give a satisfying, quality result. Custom board graphics are shown in 8 pages of colour photos.
Paperback, 120 pages

101 FREESTYLE WINDSURFING TRICKS
Sigi Hofmann

Starting with preparatory exercises, and using series photography and a breakdown of each trick into its component moves, the book makes it possible to begin with the easier ones and work up to the most daring and spectacular. The stunts here are graded according to difficulty and wind strength, and arranged in a logical sequence so that you build on the techniques already learned.
Paperback, 120 pages

RACE NAVIGATION
Stuart Quarrie

The first and *only* book on this subject. Windsurfers need to understand the strategic and tactical aspects of wind shifts and bends, currents, tide changes, speed and course made good just as much as dinghy and big-boat sailors, for whom this book was originally written. And when you go on — or back — to racing in boats, it's all here!
Hardback, 152 pages

STANFORD MARITIME
Member Company of the George Philip Group
12 Long Acre, London WC2E 9LP, U.K.